G.U.M.

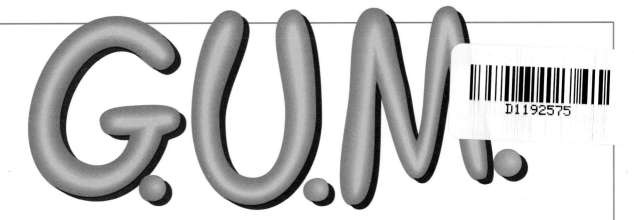

Instruction and Practice for
Grammar, Usage, and Mechanics

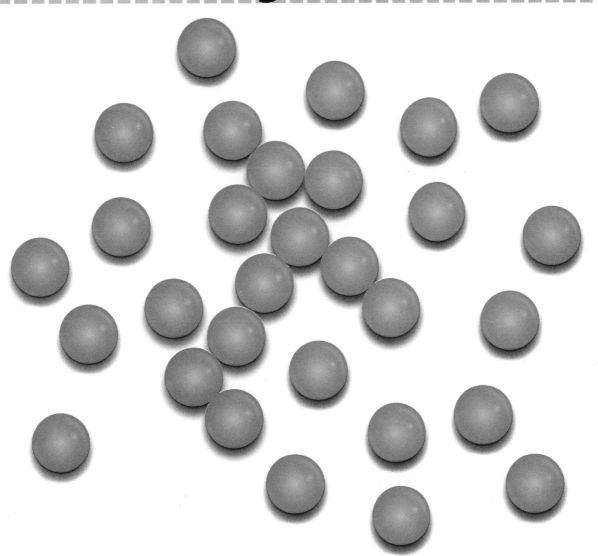

Zaner-Bloser, Inc.
Columbus, Ohio

Grade Level Consultants

CallyAnn Meulemans
Brookfield, Wisconsin

Carole Prince
St. Louis, Missouri

Pat Prosser
St. Louis, Missouri

Linda Ritchie
Birmingham, Alabama

Developed by Straight Line Editorial Development, Inc., and Zaner-Bloser, Inc.

Cover photo: Rycus Associates Photography

Illustration: Tom Kennedy

ISBN: 0-88085-808-7

Copyright © Zaner-Bloser, Inc.

Zaner-Bloser, Inc., P.O. Box 16764, Columbus, Ohio 43216-6764 (1-800-421-3018)

Printed in the United States of America

99 PO 5 4

Table of Contents

Grade 4

Unit 1 Sentence Structure

Unforgettable Folks World Leaders

Unit 2 Parts of Speech

Beasts & Critters Birds

Unit 3 Usage

The World Outside Weather

Unit 4 Grammar

Looking Back U.S. State Histories

Unit 5 Mechanics

Grab Bag Computers

Extra Practice

Unit Tests

Language Handbook

G.U.M. Indexes

Read and Discover

Was Martin Luther King, Jr., a peaceful man? Yes, he led many peaceful marches to gain rights for African Americans.

Underline the sentence that asks a question. Circle the sentence that makes a statement. Then circle each end mark.

A sentence that tells something is a statement. A command gives an order. They each end with a period. A sentence that asks something is a question. A question ends with a question mark. An exclamation shows strong feelings and ends with an exclamation point.

See Handbook Section 9

Part 1

Imagine you are living in August 1963, and a friend tells you about an important march. After each sentence, write *statement, question, exclamation,* or *command* to label the kind of sentence it is.

1. What are you doing in August? _____

2. Come march with us for equal rights. _____

3. The march will happen in Washington, D.C. _____

4. Martin Luther King, Jr., will give a speech. _____

5. Dr. King is an excellent speaker! _____

6. Meet us at the Lincoln Memorial. _____

7. Did you know that President Kennedy asked Congress

   to pass a civil rights bill? _____

8. Our march may help convince

   Congress to pass the bill. _____

Martin Luther King, Jr., fought tirelessly for civil rights.

Part 2

Write a period, a question mark, or an exclamation point at the end of each sentence. For some sentences, either a period or an exclamation point may be correct.

9. Dr. Martin Luther King, Jr., was a very brave man____

10. His home was bombed, and he was put in jail____

11. Did he decide that his work was too dangerous____

12. Though his life was threatened, he did not quit____

13. I think he was one of the greatest leaders of his time____

14. When is Martin Luther King Day____

15. We honor Dr. King on the third Monday in January____

Part 3

Use the clues to help you complete the crossword puzzle.

Across
1. A statement ends with a ____.
5. This ! is called an exclamation ____.
7. A question ends with a question ____.
8. "Are you going to school?" is a ____.

Down
2. An ____ shows strong feelings.
3. A sentence that gives an order is called a ____.
4. A ____ tells something.
6. A question might also be called an ____ sentence.

Name _____

Unforgettable Folks

Read and Discover

Susan B. Anthony/was raised in the Quaker religion.
Quakers believe in equality.

In the first sentence, the complete subject and the complete predicate are separated by /. Draw a slash (/) between the subject and the predicate in the second sentence.

The **complete subject** of a sentence tells whom or what the sentence is about. The **complete predicate** tells what happens in the sentence.

See Handbook Sections 10 and 11

Part 1

Write *S* if the underlined word or phrase is the complete subject. Write *P* if it is the complete predicate.

1. <u>Women</u> could not vote in the United States before 1920. ___

2. Susan B. Anthony <u>worked for the voting rights of women</u>. ___

3. She <u>wanted equal education for women, too</u>. ___

4. Anthony <u>formed the National Women's Suffrage Association in 1869</u>. ___

5. <u>She</u> also published a newspaper. ___

6. She <u>voted illegally in 1872</u>. ___

7. Police officers <u>arrested her</u>. ___

8. <u>Susan B. Anthony</u> fought for equality all her life. ___

9. Women's voting rights <u>became law 14 years after her death</u>. ___

10. <u>This law</u> was the 19th amendment to the U.S. Constitution. ___

The U.S. government began making $1 coins with Anthony's portrait in 1979.

Part 2 ✏️

Draw one line under the complete subject and two lines under the complete predicate of each sentence.

11. Cesar Chavez was a famous leader of Mexican American farmworkers.

12. Young Cesar's family lost their farm in Arizona.

13. The Chavez family became migrant farmworkers in California.

14. Farmworkers did not have fair wages or decent housing.

15. Chavez organized boycotts for farmworkers' rights.

16. Protesters would not buy certain farm products.

17. Farm owners lost money because of the boycotts.

18. Some of the farm owners raised wages.

Part 3 ✏️

Write a paragraph about something you think is unfair. Explain the changes you think should be made and tell who should make those changes. Then circle the complete subject in each sentence in your paragraph.

_____

_____

_____

_____

_____

_____

Name _____

Unforgettable Folks

Read  and Discover

Many wandering **tribes**/united under Genghis Khan in the late 1100s and early 1200s.

The complete subject and the complete predicate are separated by a slash (/). Which boldfaced word tells what the sentence is about? Circle it.

The complete subject tells whom or what the sentence is about. The simple subject is the most important word in the complete subject. The simple subject is a noun or pronoun. The other words in the complete subject tell about the simple subject.

See Handbook Section 10

Part 1

The complete subject of each sentence is underlined. Circle the most important word in the complete subject.

1. This famous ruler formed a huge army of warriors.

2. Genghis Khan's fierce soldiers were often cruel to prisoners.

3. Many Asian lands eventually came under his control.

4. This conqueror created the largest empire in history.

5. This brilliant ruler set up laws in these lands.

6. His important laws were called *Yasa* or *Yasak*.

7. The powerful Mongolian leader

    wanted to conquer China.

8. Genghis Khan's grandson finally

    completed the conquest of China.

In the 1200s, Genghis Khan ruled a vast empire in central Asia.

Part 2 ✏️

Write a simple subject from the word bank to complete each sentence and tell about the picture. Circle the complete subject.

horse	tutor	man	army	father	rider

9. This young _____ was named Alexander the Great.

10. His powerful _____ ruled Greece during Alexander's childhood.

11. A wise _____ taught Alexander literature and science.

12. This fearless _____ tamed Bucephalus, a horse others were afraid to ride.

13. The beautiful _____ carried Alexander to distant lands.

Alexander the Great riding Bucephalus

14. Alexander's mighty _____ fought battles in Egypt and India.

Part 3 ✏️

Look back at Part 1. Write the simple subjects you circled in the spaces below. Use the letters in circles to form a word and complete this sentence:

Even the best ___ _Q_ _U_ ___ ___ _T_ ___ _I_ ___ ___ ___ could not ride Bucephalus before Alexander tamed him.

15. __ __ __ Ⓞ __ __

16. __ __ __ __ Ⓞ __ __

17. __ __ __ Ⓞ __ __

18. __ __ __ __ __ __ __ __

19. Ⓞ __ __ __ __

20. __ __ __ __ __

21. __ __ Ⓞ __ __ __ __

22. __ __ __ Ⓞ __ Ⓞ __ __

Name _____

Unforgettable Folks

Read and Discover

Chief Joseph <u>led a band of Nez Perce people</u>.
The complete predicate in this sentence is underlined. Which word in the complete predicate tells what Chief Joseph did?

a. led **b.** band **c.** of

> The complete predicate tells what the subject of a sentence says, is, or does. The **simple predicate** is the most important verb or verb phrase in the predicate. The other words in the complete predicate tell more about this verb. For example, in the sentence *Chief Joseph fought against the U.S. Army*, the simple predicate is *fought*.

See Handbook Section 11

Part 1

Each complete predicate is underlined below. Draw a box around each simple predicate.

1. The Nez Perce <u>lived in Oregon</u>.

2. Prospectors <u>found gold on the Nez Perce lands</u>.

3. Settlers <u>wanted the land</u>.

4. A government order <u>moved the Nez Perce reservation to Idaho</u>.

5. Some Nez Perce <u>refused the order</u>.

6. They <u>left Oregon</u>.

7. Chief Joseph <u>led this group</u>.

8. Chief Joseph's warriors <u>fought government troops</u>.

9. They <u>traveled toward Canada</u>.

10. The army <u>defeated the Nez Perce warriors near the border</u>.

11. Chief Joseph <u>gave a sad and meaningful speech to his people</u>.

Chief Joseph led his people bravely during a difficult time.

Unforgettable Folks

Part 2

Complete each sentence with a simple predicate from the word bank. Add other words to make your sentences more interesting.

fought	led	raced	struggled	lasted	worried	covered	tried

12. The soldiers _____

_____.

13. The horses _____

_____.

14. Chief Joseph _____

_____.

15. The Nez Perce people _____

_____.

Part 3

Look back at the simple predicates you boxed in Part 1. Find those eleven words in this puzzle. Circle each one you find. (Answers can go across, up and down, or at an angle.)

```
S  Z  L  I  V  E  D  X  L  Q  L  E  D  X
D  T  R  Q  R  W  J  F  C  E  X  K  Q  T
R  E  E  W  K  B  L  O  K  R  F  D  J  R
M  Q  F  G  H  N  L  U  Z  L  X  T  L  A
O  B  U  E  K  J  W  N  R  G  A  V  E  V
V  G  S  K  A  G  R  D  H  Q  B  U  K  E
E  S  E  Q  J  T  V  F  O  U  G  H  T  L
D  N  D  Q  C  R  E  C  Q  L  J  Y  X  E
W  A  N  T  E  D  Q  D  W  N  K  P  R  D
```

Unforgettable Folks

Name _____

Read and Discover

Rigoberta Menchú **won** the <u>Nobel Peace Prize</u>.
She **wants** peace in Guatemala.
In the first sentence, the direct object is underlined. The direct object, *Nobel Peace Prize*, tells what Rigoberta Menchú won. Read the second sentence. Underline the direct object. (Hint: The direct object tells what Rigoberta Menchú wants.)

> The **direct object** is the noun or pronoun that receives the action of the verb. Direct objects always follow action verbs. To find the direct object, say the verb followed by "What?" or "Whom?" For example, to find the direct object in the sentence *She wants peace in Guatemala*, ask "Wants whom or what? Peace."

See Handbook Section 20

Part 1

Circle the direct object in each sentence. Draw an arrow from the underlined verb to the direct object.

1. Guatemalan Indians like Rigoberta Menchú <u>face</u> many hardships.

2. They <u>want</u> basic rights.

3. Soldiers <u>have attacked</u> many Guatemalan Indians.

4. People <u>have lost</u> their homes.

5. Rigoberta Menchú's father <u>started</u> a union.

6. Soldiers <u>killed</u> him.

7. Rigoberta Menchú <u>left</u> Guatemala in 1981.

8. She <u>wrote</u> an autobiography.

9. Her book <u>described</u> the troubles in Guatemala.

10. Many people <u>admire</u> Rigoberta Menchú.

Rigoberta Menchú works for the rights of Guatemalan Indians.

Unforgettable Folks

Part 2

Write a direct object from the word bank to complete each sentence. Draw an arrow from the verb to the direct object.

material	blouses	guitar	patterns	scene

11. Rigoberta Menchú often wears colorful _____.

12. Native Guatemalan artists weave the _____.

13. They embroider bright _____ in the cloth.

14. The artist embroidered a _____ of a band playing on

    this blouse.

15. One musician is playing a _____.

Part 3

Draw a line to match each sentence on the left with the direct object that completes it correctly.

16. Many Guatemalans play   goal!

17. Players kick the   soccer.

18. We watched a   team.

19. The Guatemalan team beat Argentina's   ball.

20. Hooray, they scored a   game.

Now write a sentence describing a game you like to play.

_____

_____

Name	_____

Unforgettable Folks

Read and Discover

The famous scientist Sir Isaac Newton died in 1727.
Write the phrase that tells when Newton died.

_____

Circle the word that begins this phrase.

A **prepositional phrase** tells about what happened in a sentence.
A prepositional phrase can tell how, when, what, how much, or where.
A prepositional phrase begins with a preposition. Some common
prepositions are *in, of, on, under,* and *to.*

See Handbook Section 19

Part 1

Underline the prepositional phrase that tells about each boldfaced word. Circle the preposition that begins each phrase. (In #6 and #7, be careful to underline only the prepositional phrase.)

1. Sir Isaac Newton is **famous** throughout the world.

2. How did Newton discover the **theory** of gravity?

3. One story says that he **sat** in his orchard.

4. An apple **fell** from a tree.

5. Newton's theory **came** in a flash.

6. Gravity **pulls** objects to the ground.

7. Newton said the same force **moves** the moon

   around the earth.

8. Newton realized that all objects **are drawn** to one another.

9. Newton's friends suggested he write a **book** about his discoveries.

10. His book **was published** in 1687.

**Sir Isaac Newton was the first person
to understand the force of gravity.**

Unforgettable Folks

Part 2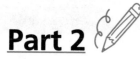

Write a prepositional phrase to finish each sentence. Begin each phrase with a word from the word bank. (The first one was done for you.) Circle the preposition in each phrase.

into	across	on	over	under

11. Frank walked slowly _____ (across) the bridge _____.

12. He tossed a smooth pebble _____.

13. Gravity made the pebble fall _____.

14. The pebble made water splash _____.

15. Then a frog jumped _____.

Part 3

Use prepositions to complete the puzzle. Use the clues to help you.

Across
1. My class saw a gravity exhibit __ the science museum.
2. We stayed __ two hours.
5. A feather floated __ an air tube.
6. A model of the solar system hung from the ceiling. We walked __ it.
7. The planets were __ our heads.
8. I walked __ Pluto all the way to the sun!

Down
1. Earth was rotating __ the sun.
3. I stood in the center so the sun was right __ my head.
4. Stars were spattered __ the ceiling.
5. We threw balls __ a bucket.

Name _____

Unforgettable Folks

Read and Discover

Mother Teresa has cared for the poor and the ill for many years. Founded a religious order. These nuns were named the Missionaries of Charity. The members of this group feed the hungry and help nurse the sick.

Underline the sentence in the paragraph that does not tell a complete thought. What is it missing? _____

A sentence tells a complete thought. A sentence needs a subject and a predicate. A **sentence fragment** is a group of words that is missing either a subject or a predicate. A sentence fragment is also called an **incomplete sentence**.

See Handbook Sections 9 and 13

Part 1

Circle five incomplete sentences below. Rewrite each one so it tells a complete thought.

Mother Teresa was born in Macedonia in 1910. Wanted to help people. She moved to Calcutta, India, in 1928. Sick people who lived in the slums. Since 1950, her organization has run shelters, hospitals, and schools for the poor. Has branches in other countries. Stories about Mother Teresa in newspapers. Winner of the Nobel Peace Prize in 1979.

1. _____

2. _____

_____

3. _____

4. _____

_____

5. _____

_____

Part 2

Add words to each phrase to make complete sentences. Write the sentences on the lines.

6. Mother Teresa _____

_____

7. rushed to bring medicine _____

_____

8. helped many people _____

_____

_____

9. The Missionaries of Charity _____

_____

_____

Mother Teresa helps the sick and needy.

10. won the Nobel Peace Prize _____

_____

Part 3

Write two complete sentences about something you would like to do to help people. Make sure each sentence has a subject and a predicate.

11. _____

_____

12. _____

_____

Name _____

Unforgettable Folks

Read  and Discover

    a. Sojourner Truth worked to gain the vote for women and to end slavery.

    b. Sojourner Truth was an important woman.

Which sentence gives more information? _____

Sentences that include details, descriptive words, and words with exact meanings **give more information**. For example, *brave* tells more than *great.* **Remember to use this information when you speak, too.**

See Handbook Sections 15, 18, and 19

Part 1

Draw a star by the sentence in each pair that gives more information.

1. **a.** Sojourner Truth had known bad times, and she wanted to help others. ___

    b. Truth had been enslaved herself, and when she became free she worked for the abolition of slavery. ___

2. **a.** Truth spoke against slavery, even though her views made some Southerners angry. ___

    b. Truth noticed injustice, and she talked about it. ___

3. **a.** No African American woman had spoken in public against slavery before Truth. ___

    b. Truth did things no one had done before. ___

4. **a.** During the Civil War, Truth collected clothing and food for African American troops. ___

    b. Truth worked hard during the Civil War. ___

Sojourner Truth traveled to make speeches against slavery in the 1800s.

5. **a.** Important people listened to Truth. ___

    b. Truth visited Abraham Lincoln at the White House in 1864 and spoke with him. ___

6. **a.** Truth traveled and said what she felt. ___

    b. Truth walked hundreds of miles, spreading a message of peace and justice. ___

 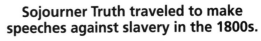

Part 2

Write four sentences about someone you admire. Use words from the word bank and your own words. Include exact words and descriptive words.

patient	clever	daring	struggled	adventure	travels

7. _____

_____

8. _____

_____

9. _____

_____

10. _____

_____

Part 3

The phrases in the right-hand column say more than the phrases in the left-hand column. Draw lines to match the phrases.

11. a good smell   the feeling of loneliness you get when a friend moves away

12. a sad feeling   the icy air that stung her face and hands

13. a cold day outside   a fragrance of cinnamon and fresh bread baking

Use one phrase in the right-hand column to write a detailed sentence.

_____

_____

Name _____

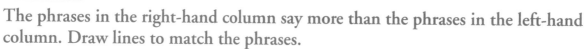

Unforgettable Folks

Read and Discover

Many people felt that Charlie Chaplin was the funniest actor in the world.

His movies made people laugh, but Chaplin was also a serious filmmaker.

Draw a star by the sentence that contains two short sentences.

What joins the two short sentences? _____

> A **compound sentence** is made up of two simple sentences. A simple sentence has one subject and one predicate. To write a compound sentence, include a comma (,) followed by *and, but,* or *or.* Joining words like *and, but,* and *or* are called *conjunctions*.
>
> **See Handbook Sections 12 and 21**

Part 1

Underline the compound sentences below. Circle the comma and the conjunction in each sentence you underline. (1–8)

First Charlie Chaplin made silent movies. His audience couldn't hear jokes, but Chaplin entertained them with his silly actions. Chaplin might fall down for a laugh, or he might make a funny face.

In many movies Chaplin carried a bamboo cane, and he often wore oversized shoes. His coat was too small, and his pants were too large. He wore a beat-up hat, and he walked with a shuffle. He didn't have much money, but he never became too discouraged. His white gloves gave him an elegant look. His character was called "The Tramp."

Chaplin controlled every part of his movies. He wrote the scripts, and he directed the filming. Chaplin worked very hard, but he made acting look easy.

Charlie Chaplin made "The Tramp" famous.

Unforgettable Folks

Part 2

Circle the simple subject in each sentence. Underline each simple predicate. Rewrite each pair of sentences as one compound sentence.

9. Walt Disney studied art as a boy. He became a cartoonist. _____

_____

10. He started his own cartoon studio. He created Mickey Mouse. _____

_____

_____

11. In 1937, Disney made <u>Snow White and the Seven Dwarfs</u>. It became a big hit.

_____

_____

12. We could rent a videotape of <u>Snow White</u>. Maybe you would rather rent <u>Pocahontas</u>.

_____

_____

Part 3

Unscramble the words to make one compound sentence. Write the new sentence below. There is more than one way to rewrite it.

Pocahontas brings the two groups together, the colonists and the Native Americans see each other as savages at first, in the movie <u>Pocahontas</u>, but.

_____

_____

_____

Name _____

Unforgettable Folks

Read and Discover

Leonardo da Vinci was a talented painter he also designed flying machines.

Leonardo da Vinci created paintings for others, but he also filled notebooks with drawings of his own inventions.

Circle the incorrect sentence. How many sentences are in it? _____

A **run-on sentence** is a compound sentence that is missing a comma and a conjunction. A **comma splice** is a compound sentence that has a comma but is missing a conjunction. To fix each type of incorrect sentence, add what is missing, or make two separate sentences.

See Handbook Sections 12 and 13

Part 1

Write *C* after each compound sentence, *RO* after each run-on, and *CS* after each comma splice.

1. Leonardo sketched many great ideas, but he could only build some of them. _____

2. He drew an idea for a parachute, he named it a "tent roof." _____

3. The first successful parachute jump was made in 1783 that was 264 years after Leonardo's death. _____

4. Leonardo wrote about his inventions backward, you could read the words with a mirror. _____

5. He designed a flying machine, he also designed a movable bridge. _____

This writing must be read in a mirror, like da Vinci's notes.

6. Leonardo was a careful observer, and many topics interested him. _____

7. At that time few people understood fossils Leonardo studied them. _____

8. Leonardo studied the human body, he made many detailed drawings of muscles and bones. _____

Part 2

Rewrite the run-on sentences and the comma splices correctly. There is more than one way to rewrite each one.

9. One painting shows a woman she seems to be about to smile.

_____

_____

10. The painting is called <u>Mona Lisa</u>, many people have admired the woman's mysterious smile.

_____

_____

11. Leonardo showed the woman's head and shoulders, he also showed her folded hands.

_____

_____

12. This way of painting portraits was new it made people look more natural.

_____

_____

Part 3

Write a compound sentence that compares two people you read about in Unit 1. Be sure NOT to write a run-on sentence or a comma splice!

_____

_____

_____

Name _____

Unforgettable Folks

Proofreading Others' Writing

Read this report about Clara Barton and find the mistakes. Use the proofreading marks below to show how each mistake should be fixed.

Proofreading Marks

Mark	Means	Example
℘	take away	Clara Barton did helped people.
∧	add	Clara Barton helped. ^people
≡	make into a capital letter	Clara barton helped people.
/	make into a lowercase letter	Clara Barton helped People.
⊙	add a period	Clara Barton helped people⊙
(sp)	fix spelling	Clara Barton halped people.

Clara Barton

Have you heard of Clara Barton. Born in 1821. Clara Barton cared for hundreds of sick and wounded soldiers.

During the the Civil War, many soldiers were injured. There weren't enough hospitals for the wounded soldiers. Conditions were dirty. Very little medicine. Many unnecessary deaths happened because of these poor conditions. Clara Barton walked onto battlefields she cared for the wounded there? She showed grate courage.

After the war, Barton traveled to switzerland? There she learned about the International Red Cross this group helped injured soldiers. Barton returned home, she founded the American Red Cross. Her group helped soldiers, but it also helped other people in need. Especially victims of disasters. Barton's group took care of the survivors of a terrible flood. The American Red Cross is still helping peeple today.

Proofreading Your Own Writing

You can use the list below to help you find and fix mistakes in your own writing. Write the titles of your own stories or reports in the blanks on top of the chart. Then use the questions to check your work. Make a check mark (✓) in each box after you have checked that item.

Titles

Proofreading Checklist for Unit 1

Does each sentence end with the right mark (period, question mark, exclamation point)?				
Does each sentence have both a subject and a predicate? Are there any sentence fragments?				
Have I avoided run-on sentences and comma splices?				
Does each sentence provide specific and detailed information?				

Also Remember . . .

Does each sentence begin with a capital letter?				
Have I spelled each word correctly?				
Have I used commas correctly?				

Your Own List
Use this space to write your own list of things to check in your writing.

Name

Unforgettable Folks

Kinds of Sentences

Add the correct end mark for each sentence.

1. Have you ever heard of Ella Fitzgerald__

2. What a marvelous voice she has__

3. She began singing with famous jazz orchestras in 1935__

4. Look for her CDs in a music store__

Subjects and Predicates

Underline the complete subject in each sentence. Draw a box around the simple subject.

5. The famous and talented Tito Puente plays the timbales.

6. This musical instrument is a kind of kettledrum.

Underline the complete predicate. Draw a box around the simple predicate.

7. Tito Puente's hands move very fast over his drums.

8. He plays music with Latin rhythms.

9. People dance the mambo to his music.

Direct Objects

Circle the direct object in each sentence.

10. Itzhak Perlman studied music as a boy in Israel.

11. Perlman plays the violin.

12. This famous musician has won many prizes.

Prepositions

Use one of these prepositions to complete each sentence: *into, for, in.*

13. Mikhail Baryshnikov performs _____ huge audiences.

14. This great ballet dancer often leaps high _____ the air.

15. Baryshnikov was born _____ Riga, Latvia.

Better Sentences

Rewrite this sentence to tell more.

16. My state is an interesting place. _____

_____

Fragments, Run-ons, and Comma Splices

Underline the two incomplete sentences. Rewrite each one as a complete sentence.

Art Tatum was one of the greatest jazz piano players. Born in Toledo, Ohio. Tatum never wrote any of his own songs, but he played the piano in a way that dazzled those who heard him. He played with many famous people during his lifetime. His death in 1956.

17. _____

_____

18. _____

Write *C* by each compound sentence, *RO* by each run-on, and *CS* by each comma splice. Use this mark (^) to add a conjunction to correct each run-on and comma splice.

19. Martha Graham was a famous dancer, she created modern dance. _____

20. She was graceful, but sometimes she moved clumsily on purpose. _____

21. Graham expressed feelings with her body her dances were very unusual. _____

22. Graham changed the world of dance, and her ideas are still important today. _____

Name _____

Unforgettable Folks

FAMILY LEARNING OPPORTUNITIES

In Unit 1 of *G.U.M.* we are learning about different types of sentences and about the important parts of a sentence. The activities on this page give extra practice with some of the concepts we're learning. You can help your child use the information he or she is learning in school by choosing one or more activities to complete with your child at home.

Treasure Hunt (Prepositional Phrases)

Work with your child to create a treasure hunt. Follow these directions.

1. Think of five to ten places to hide clues. You could hide them in closets, under vases, under beds, or in cupboards.
2. Write a set of clues that will lead finders from one hiding place to the next. (Each clue that is found should direct finders to the next clue.)
3. Decide what the "treasure" will be. It could be a bowl of popcorn, a new set of crayons, or a plate of cookies.

Make sure you use a prepositional phrase in each clue. Each prepositional phrase in these example clues is in dark type.

Example	Look **in Tricia's closet.** Look **under Robert's bed.** Find something red **in the bathroom cabinet.**

Happy Hunting!

Sentence Scramble (Complete Subject and Complete Predicate)

Ask your child to choose sentences from favorite books or magazines. Then help your child to copy each sentence on a card. Cut each card apart between the sentence's complete subject and complete predicate. (The subject is the part of a sentence that tells whom or what the sentence is about. The predicate is the part of a sentence that tells what happens.) Make one pile of "subject cards" and one pile of "predicate cards." Mix up each pile. Recombine subjects and predicates at random to make funny new sentences.

Example	Large robots/work in factories. Cherry jelly beans/taste the best.

Changes to	Large robots/taste the best. Cherry jelly beans/work in factories.

Unforgettable Folks

Curtain Up! (Kinds of Sentences)

Invite your child to write a conversation between two characters using each type of sentence (statement, question, command, exclamation) at least once. (A statement tells a fact. A question asks for information. A command gives an order. An exclamation shows strong feeling, and ends with an exclamation point.) Act out the scene with your child.

Who Did What to Whom? (Direct Objects)

Have your child look through magazines to find interesting action photos. Ask your child to write a caption to go with his or her favorite photo. Encourage your child to include a direct object (the word that receives the action of the verb) in each sentence of the caption.

| Example | The player hit the **ball**. |

Now and Then (Compound Sentences)

Ask your child to write a few sentences comparing his or her life in first grade with his or her life now. Encourage your child to use compound sentences to describe how things are the same and how things are different. (A compound sentence is two sentences made into one sentence and joined by *and, or,* or *but.*)

| Example | Back then I had short hair, but now my hair is long.
I liked yogurt then, and I still do. |

Animal Watch (Prepositional Phrases)

With your child, watch wildlife in your area. (Even busy city streets are often home to birds, squirrels, and raccoons.) Keep a journal of what you see for one week. Ask your child to sketch each creature you saw and to write a sentence about where it lives. Encourage your child to use prepositional phrases to tell where each creature lives. (Prepositional phrases begin with words such as *to, in, by, under, over,* and *through.*)

| Examples | A red robin lives **in a tree**.
Two rabbits live **under a log**. |

Name _____

Read and Discover

A penguin is a **bird** that stands on two short **legs**. It cannot **fly**, but it is a graceful swimmer. Most penguins live where it is very cold. Penguins are quite comfortable on ice and snow.

Circle each boldfaced word that names a person, place, or thing. Then circle two other words in the paragraph that name people, places, or things.

A **noun** is a word that names a person, place, or thing.

See Handbook Section 14

Part 1

Circle the boldfaced word in each sentence that is a noun.

1. The color of a bird's **feathers** often **blends** with its surroundings.

2. This makes it **difficult** for **enemies** to find the bird.

3. A bird that **lives** in a cold, snowy **region** might have white feathers.

4. It **would** be difficult to see a white bird against the **snow**.

5. Most **parrots** and macaws live in warm, **wet** regions among colorful flowers and bright green leaves.

6. Even though these birds' feathers are **very** brightly colored, they match their **surroundings**.

7. Many birds that live in the forest have **brown** feathers that blend in with the **shadows**.

Macaws are sometimes kept as pets.

Beasts & Critters

Part 2

Choose the noun from the word bank that best completes each sentence. Write the word in the blank.

group	ground	pond	liquid	geese	activity	dirt	birds	sound	flock

8. Doris watched the _____ fly over the pond.

9. They flew in a _____ with one goose leading the way.

10. The honking _____ faded as the geese flew away.

11. A light layer of snow covered the _____.

12. Soon the _____ would be covered with ice.

Part 3

Figure out the answer to each riddle. Each answer is a noun that names a bird.

13. I'm a good swimmer. My name rhymes with "truck." I'm a ___ ___ ___ ___.

14. My name rhymes with "carrot." I can be taught to talk.

    I'm a ___ ___ ___ ___ ___ ___.

15. I hunt at night. People think I'm wise, but I say, "*Who* knows?"

    I'm an ___ ___ ___.

16. I am the color of coal. My sound is "Caw! Caw!" I'm a ___ ___ ___ ___.

17. I am the largest bird there is. I have a long neck. I run but don't fly.

    I'm an ___ ___ ___ ___ ___ ___ ___.

18. I live in a barnyard. Many people eat the eggs I lay.

    I'm a ___ ___ ___ ___ ___ ___ ___.

Name _____

Beasts & Critters

Read and Discover

John J. Audubon was an **artist** who lived in the 1800s. He was one of the first people to study and paint the **birds** of **North America**. Audubon started painting in Philadelphia when he was about 18 years old. His first book of paintings was published in Scotland in the 1830s. He became famous for his lifelike paintings of birds.

Circle each group of boldfaced words that names one particular person, place, or thing. Then find and circle three other nouns that name particular people, places, or things.

A common noun names any person, place, or thing. A proper noun names a particular person, place, or thing. Proper nouns begin with a capital letter.

See Handbook Section 14

Part 1

Circle the proper noun in each sentence. Some of the proper nouns are groups of words.

1. The National Audubon Society was started in 1905.

2. This conservation group was named after the artist John J. Audubon.

3. The group is the oldest and largest organization of its kind in North America.

4. In July our teacher went to a workshop presented by the society.

5. The workshop was held at a camp in Maine.

6. This conservation group has children's clubs in Australia and many other countries.

7. The national headquarters is in New York City.

John J. Audubon

Part 2 ✏️

Rewrite each sentence. Change each boldfaced word or phrase into a proper noun that names a particular person, place, or thing. If you like, invent proper nouns to use.

8. My brother and I joined **a bird-watching club.** _____

_____

9. **My brother** wanted to see all of the birds in Audubon's book. _____

_____

10. The club members went to **a lake** to watch water birds. _____

_____

11. In **the city park** we watched pigeons, robins, and blue jays. _____

_____

12. **Our club president** says we may go to Florida to watch wood storks. _____

_____

Part 3 ✏️

Imagine that you can start your own club. What would you name it? What would your club be interested in? Where might you go for a club field trip? Write three sentences about your new club. Don't forget to capitalize the name of your club and any other proper nouns you use.

_____

_____

_____

_____

Name _____

Beasts & Critters

Read and Discover

The Australian satin **bowerbird** collects anything that is blue. It decorates its nest with blue things. It might collect **marbles**, **flowers**, or pieces of a broken **dish**.

Circle each boldfaced noun that names more than one person, place, or thing.

> A **singular noun** names one thing. A **plural noun** names more than one. Most singular nouns become plural when you add *s* (*dog/dogs*). If a singular noun ends in *s*, *x*, *ch*, or *sh*, add *es* to make it a plural noun (*tax/taxes*). If a singular noun ends in *y*, change the *y* to *i* before adding *es* (*daisy/daisies*). If a singular noun ends in *f*, change the *f* to *v* to form the plural (*shelf/shelves*).

See Handbook Section 25

Part 1

Decide whether each boldfaced word is a singular or plural noun. Circle the plural nouns. Draw a line under the singular nouns. (1–11)

The **life** of the male satin bowerbird is spent collecting blue **objects** and painting his

bower. A **bower** is a place male **bowerbirds**

use to attract a mate. The male paints

the inside of the bower with a paint

made of charcoal and the **juice** from

special **berries**. He makes a **paintbrush**

from a piece of bark and then paints

the **twigs** of his bower. **Persons** who live

near satin **bowerbirds** quickly learn not

Bowerbirds live in Australia, New Zealand, and New Guinea.

to grow blue **flowers** or use blue things outside, because a bowerbird might steal them.

Beasts & Critters

Part 2 ✏️

Rewrite each boldfaced singular noun as a plural noun.

12. I saw a **berry** on a **vine**. _____ _____

13. The **bowerbird** swept down swiftly to pick the **fruit**.

    _____ _____

14. The **bird** took a blue **toothbrush** I left outside overnight.

    _____ _____

15. The bowerbird decorated his **perch** with **moss**.

    _____ _____

16. I wondered how much that **bird** has collected in its **life**.

    _____ _____

17. Its **bower** contains an amazing **mix** of things.

    _____ _____

Part 3 ✏️

Write a sentence about what you see. Use singular and plural nouns.

_____

_____

_____

_____

Name _____

Beasts & Critters

Read and Discover

Wood storks build **their** nests in swampy areas in Florida. **They** work in pairs to build nests.

The pronoun *their* refers to the wood storks. What does the pronoun *they* refer to? _____

Personal pronouns include the words *I, me, you, we, us, he, him, she, her, they, them,* and *it*. These words can be used in place of names of people and things. Possessive pronouns include the words *my, your, his, her, its, their,* and *our*. These show ownership (*my dog; their phone number*). **Remember to use this information when you speak, too.**

See Handbook Section 16

Part 1

Circle the boldfaced word in each sentence that is a pronoun. Write a check mark above each possessive pronoun.

1. The wood stork uses **its** long beak **to** catch fish and frogs.

2. The wood stork's long, **thin** legs help **it** wade in the Florida swamps.

3. The male and female wood stork build

   their nest together.

4. **They** collect thin sticks **for** the nest.

5. The female lays three or four eggs, and

   both **parents** help sit on **them**.

6. When a wood stork is **born, it** has a yellow beak.

7. **Its** body is **covered** with soft white down.

8. When wood **storks** are older, **their** beaks turn dark gray.

Wood storks sometimes fly up to 50 miles to find food.

Beasts & Critters

Part 2

Choose a pronoun from the word bank that could replace each boldfaced word.
Write that pronoun on the line.

her	they	it	its	we	them	our	their

9. One popular myth about storks is that **storks** deliver human babies. _____

10. The only babies storks deliver are **the storks'** own chicks. _____

11. My aunt says a few storks nest on **my aunt's** farm. _____

12. A baby stork can make a lot of noise when **a baby stork** wants **a baby stork's**

   mother's attention. _____   _____

Part 3

Use the clues to complete the crossword puzzle. Each answer is a pronoun.

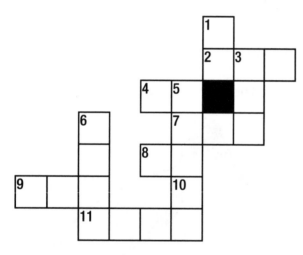

Across

2. __ are my best friend!
4. I picked up the book, and then I put __ down.
7. Rhonda asked if I would carry __ coat.
8. My family and I are going to Florida, and I know __ will have a good time.
9. Melanie said that __ would call me.
10. __ am fine, thanks!
11. You must be very proud of __ good grades.

Down

1. Mom told me that it was __ turn to clear the table.
3. We had a wonderful time on __ vacation.
5. The family is eating __ dinner.
6. I told them that __ didn't need to call me back.

Color the personal pronouns red and the possessive pronouns blue.

Name _____

Beasts & Critters

Read and Discover

Who knows how ducks keep dry in the water? **Mari** knows. She looked up *Ducks* in an encyclopedia.

What do ducks put on their feathers to waterproof them? They use a **waxy oil** made by their bodies.

Which are female? The **ducks with brown feathers** are female.

Circle the boldfaced words that show a question is being asked. Underline the boldfaced words that answer each question.

Words that introduce questions are called interrogative pronouns. *Who*, *what*, and *which* are interrogative pronouns. *Who* is used to ask questions about people. *What* is used to ask questions about places or ideas. *Which* is used when the answer to the question is a choice between two or more things.

See Handbook Section 16

Part 1

Circle the interrogative pronoun that belongs in each sentence.

1. (Who/What) has seen the ducks on the Russian River?

2. (What/Which) are mallards, the brown ducks or the green ones?

3. (What/Which) are the ducks doing when they stand up tall and flap their wings?

4. (Which/What) are the males, the brightly colored ones or the brown ones?

5. (Which/What) feed on the bottoms of ponds?

6. (Which/What) do the baby ducks eat?

7. (Who/What) saw a flock of ducks flying in a V pattern?

8. (What/Which) are ducklings able to do as soon as they hatch?

Some ducks use their long necks and bills to get food from the bottoms of rivers and lakes.

Beasts & Critters

Part 2

Write a question to go with each answer. Begin each question with *Who, What,* or *Which*.

9. _____

   The canvasback, the redhead, and the ringneck ducks all dive for their food.

10. _____

   Mr. Crowley said he would buy some duck eggs from the farm.

11. _____

   Ducks eat water plants.

12. _____

   The male ducks are the ones with the brightly colored feathers.

Part 3

What do you want to know about ducks? Pretend you can interview a duck. Write some questions you could ask. Begin each question with *Who, What,* or *Which.*

13. _____

   _____

14. _____

   _____

15. _____

   _____

Name _____

Beasts & Critters

Read and Discover

An albatross **is** a clumsy, curious sea bird. Some people call albatrosses *gooney birds.* An albatross **chooses** a mate for life. These birds **are** affectionate with their mates. They **make** a lot of clacking noises together.

Underline the boldfaced verbs that tell what albatrosses do. Circle the boldfaced verbs that link subjects with words that tell about the subjects.

An **action verb** tells what the subject of a sentence does. (*She **shares** her toys.*) A **linking verb** links the subject with words that tell what the subject is like. (*She **is** friendly.*) Linking verbs include *am, is, are, was, were, become,* and *seem.*

See Handbook **Section 17**

Part 1

The verbs in these sentences are boldfaced. Circle each linking verb. Underline each action verb.

1. Gooney birds **are** curious creatures.

2. They **examine** any object or person that is new to them.

3. The gooney bird's body **is** mostly white.

4. A gooney bird's wings **are** up to 11 feet long from tip to tip.

5. Gooney birds **glide** in the sky for long periods of time.

6. The gooney bird's beak **is** quite long.

7. They **dance** in circles with their beaks in the air.

8. Pairs of gooney birds **stay** together for life.

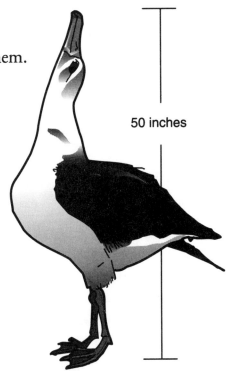

50 inches

An adult gooney bird is as tall as a small child!

Beasts & Critters

Part 2

Write about a bird you have seen. Write two sentences with action verbs and two sentences with linking verbs. You can use the words in the word bank if you want.

are	walk	fly	is

9. _____

10. _____

11. _____

12. _____

Part 3

Find three hidden action verbs, three hidden linking verbs, and three hidden nouns. Circle all the words you find. Write the verbs in the correct column.

B	E	A	K	M	G	I	S	Z	A	R	E
T	C	A	T	C	H	Q	T	B	F	J	R
B	Z	W	I	H	U	W	J	Q	K	B	L
F	Q	P	G	T	Y	E	B	G	P	I	Q
J	A	S	E	Z	T	G	J	L	W	R	I
L	E	A	P	Y	N	G	T	I	Q	D	F
R	S	E	J	Q	M	F	M	D	D	A	S
M	W	E	R	E	I	J	T	E	H	R	K

Action Verbs   **Linking Verbs**

13. _____   16. _____

14. _____   17. _____

15. _____   18. _____

Name _____

Beasts & Critters

Read  and Discover

Homer the pigeon **is** (flying) to his home loft. He **was released** 100 miles from home. He **can find** his home easily.

Circle the most important boldfaced verb in each sentence. Underline the other boldfaced verb. One has been done for you.

The **main verb** is the most important verb in a sentence. A **helping verb** comes before the main verb.

See Handbook Section 17

Part 1

In each sentence, circle the main verb and underline the helping verb.

1. Homing pigeons are raised for a special purpose.

2. People have used pigeons as messengers for thousands of years.

3. Some homing pigeons are trained as racers.

4. These birds may fly over 600 miles in a race.

5. Landmarks such as mountains and lakes may guide homing pigeons to their homes.

6. Homing pigeons can find their way through unfamiliar areas, too.

7. Perhaps homing pigeons are guided by the sun's position.

8. Some homing pigeons have become lost in foggy or cloudy weather.

9. Older birds may race better in bad weather.

Some homing pigeons have flown as fast as 60 miles per hour.

Part 2

Rewrite each sentence by adding a helping verb from the word bank. Change the main verb if you need to.

will	can	has	have

10. Jonas trained his pigeon Tweeter. _____

    _____

11. Tweeter carries tiny, rolled-up messages in a capsule on her leg. _____

    _____

    _____

12. Tweeter finds her way home from many miles away. _____

    _____

Part 3

Use the clues to help you complete the puzzle with helping verbs. You will need to use some helping verbs more than once.

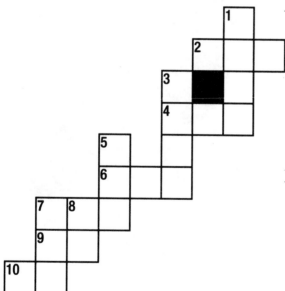

Across

2. I __ go to the race if I get all my work done.
4. They __ going to the race no matter what.
6. We __ going to a race this Saturday.
7. Last week Mitch __ planning to go to the race.
9. I __ getting ready to go to the race right now.
10. Tweeter __ getting ready to race right now.

Down

1. I __ seen Tweeter race many times.
3. My friends __ seen Tweeter race, too.
5. Veronica __ trained birds for years.
7. Yesterday she __ getting ready for a big race.
8. I __ going to watch the race today.

Name _____

Read and Discover

Eagles have **powerful** wings. They glide **gracefully** above the mountains.

Circle the boldfaced word that describes how eagles glide. Underline the boldfaced word that describes what eagles' wings are like.

An **adjective** usually describes a noun or a pronoun. It tells what the noun or pronoun is like. An **adverb** that ends in -ly usually tells about a verb. It tells how something is done, or how often it is done.

Remember to use this information when you speak, too.

See Handbook **Sections 15 and 18**

Part 1

List all of the adjectives and adverbs in these paragraphs. Two have been listed for you.

The eagle is a skillful hunter. Eagles usually hunt during the day. They fly silently over fields and rivers. They search for prey with their sharp eyes. Eagles dive swiftly. They carefully carry the food back to their hungry chicks.

Eagles that live in tropical regions generally eat mammals such as monkeys. Those that live in grassy regions eat rabbits and squirrels.

Eagles grasp their prey in sharp talons.

Adjectives

1. skillful

2. _____

3. _____

4. _____

5. _____

Adverbs

6. usually

7. _____

8. _____

9. _____

10. _____

Part 2

Choose an adverb or an adjective from the lists below to complete each sentence.

Adjectives	Adverbs
skillful	hungrily
sharp	occasionally
tall	swiftly

11. Bald eagles build their *aerie*, or nest, in a _____ tree.

12. The female sits on the eggs most of the time, though the male

    _____ takes a turn, too.

13. When the eggs hatch, the eagle chicks cry _____ for food.

14. The parents are _____ hunters.

15. They use their _____ claws to clutch their prey.

16. They _____ carry the food back to their chicks.

Part 3

The answer to each riddle is an adverb ending in *-ly*. The letters in the circles spell the name of a type of pen made from a feather. Solve the riddles and write the mystery word.

17. If you don't want to be heard, you step (Q) U __ __ T __ __.

18. If you are calling for help, you yell L __ (__) D __ __.

19. If you are angry, you speak A __ G __ (__) __ __.

20. If you want to get somewhere fast, you run Q __ __ __ K (__) __.

21. If you are glad about something, you smile H __ P __ __ (__) __.

What is the mystery word? ___ ___ ___ ___ ___

Name _____

Beasts & Critters

Read and Discover

The Canada geese flew **over the lake**.
Underline the boldfaced words that tell where the geese flew.
Circle the first word in that phrase.

A **preposition** tells about the relationship between a noun or a pronoun and another word in a sentence. Prepositions include words such as *on, above, in, below,* and *of*. The preposition, and the words that follow it, make a **prepositional phrase**. Some prepositional phrases help tell where something is.

See Handbook Section 19

Part 1

Underline the prepositional phrase in each sentence. Circle the preposition that begins that phrase.

1. The Canada goose has white patches on its cheeks.

2. Canada geese build nests on mounds.

3. They often use mounds in marshes.

4. The female lays several eggs in the nest.

5. Geese glide smoothly across a lake's surface.

6. Some Canada geese spend the summer months in central Canada.

7. Then they fly south to the Gulf of Mexico.

8. They spend the winter in that warm, sunny region.

9. Some Canada geese live in Europe, too.

Canada geese fly thousands of miles when they migrate.

Part 2

Imagine that you were in a boat on a lake and a flock of Canada geese flew by. Complete each sentence below using a prepositional phrase. Begin each phrase with one of these prepositions: *on, over, under, across, in, by, with, above.*

10. I saw geese flying _____.

11. One goose landed _____.

12. It swam _____.

Part 3

Fill in the puzzle with prepositions that tell where. Use the clues to help you. You will use some prepositions more than once.

Across

2. The geese landed __ the surface of the lake.
4. Their feet went __ the water.
5. Renée saw several large colorful fish __ the pier.
7. She rode her bike __ the bridge.
8. Then she took off her shoes and waded __ the lake.

Down

1. How long does it take to ride a bike all __ the lake?
3. Renée stepped __ the doorway and into the shed.
4. Her bike was __ the shed.
6. Her brother's bike was right __ hers.

Name _____

Read and Discover

Robins eat insects **and** fruit. The male robin has bright red feathers on his chest, **but** the female is less colorful.

Circle the boldfaced word that connects two words within a sentence. Underline the boldfaced word that connects two shorter sentences.

And, or, and *but* are called **conjunctions**. They connect words and phrases within a sentence. *And, or,* and *but* can also connect two shorter sentences and form one longer sentence. When you join two sentences with a conjunction, add a comma before the conjunction.

See Handbook Section 21

Part 1

Underline the conjunction in each sentence.

1. Some robins fly south and escape the winter chill.

2. Other robins stay in one place all year long and brave the cold weather.

3. The weather is cold, but these birds usually survive.

4. They eat seeds, berries, and other fruit.

5. Sometimes food is scarce, but people can help robins by putting food in bird feeders.

6. In the spring, a male robin claims a territory and finds a mate.

7. Male robins sometimes fight over a certain territory, but only one of them can claim it.

Robins often live near people.

8. In the summer, robins eat worms, caterpillars, and other bugs.

Part 2

Use *and, or,* or *but* to rewrite each pair of sentences as one sentence. There is more than one way to rewrite each sentence.

9. Some robins nest in trees. Some nest in barns. _____

_____

10. Robins may live in the city. They may live in the country. _____

_____

11. Most robins do not share their nests. A pair of robins and a pair of cardinals once

built a nest together in Ohio. _____

_____

_____

12. A robin's eggs are usually blue-green. A robin's eggs may have brown speckles.

_____

_____

Part 3

Each sentence in the left column can be connected to a sentence on the right with *and, but,* or *or.* Draw a line to match sentences. On the line, write a comma and the conjunction you would use to join the sentences.

13. Robins are members of the thrush family   we can draw cardinals instead.

14. Some people adopt wild baby birds   like most thrushes they have beautiful voices.

15. We can draw robins   adopting wild birds is not a good idea.

Name _____

Proofreading Others' Writing

Read this report about peacocks and find the mistakes. Use the proofreading marks below to show how each mistake should be corrected.

Proofreading Marks

Mark	Means	Example
⌞	take away	The nightingale sang in the the tree.
∧	add	The nightingale sang in the tree.
≡	make into a capital letter	the nightingale sang in the tree.
/	make into a lowercase letter	The Nightingale sang in the tree.
⊙	add a period	The nightingale sang in the tree⊙
sp	fix spelling	The nitengale sang in the tree.

Pretty as a Peacock

Peacocks are known for their large size and beautiful feathers. *Peacock* is the name for the male peafowl. The Female is called a peahen Her fethers are not very brightly colored.

The peacock's feathers are the colors of jewels. He has bright blue-green feathers on his neck and breast. the feathers on belly are deep purple. The most striking part of a peacock is his train. Long feathers grow out of the peacock's back? Some of these feather are almost five times the length of his body! The peacock uses this train during the mating season He graceful spreads his train into a beautiful fan, and then he struts slow in front of the peahen.

Human being have been fascinated with peacocks for thousands of years. The peacock was mentioned in an ancient Greek play, and many people in the Past considered peacocks to be priceless treasureses. Wild peacocks are found in india, Malaysia, and a few other countrys. Tame peacocks are found all over the world.

Proofreading Your Own Writing

You can use the list below to help you find and fix mistakes in your own writing. Write the titles of your own stories or reports in the blanks on top of the chart. Then use the questions to check your work. Make a check mark (✔) in each box after you have checked that item.

Proofreading Checklist for Unit 2

	Titles			
Have I capitalized proper nouns?				
Have I used singular and plural nouns correctly?				
Have I used adjectives and adverbs correctly?				
Have I used action verbs and linking verbs correctly?				

Also Remember . . .

Does each sentence begin with a capital letter?				
Does each sentence end with the right mark?				
Have I spelled each word correctly?				
Have I used commas correctly?				

Your Own List

Use this space to write your own list of things to check in your writing.

Name _____

Beasts & Critters

Nouns

Circle the boldfaced word in each sentence that is a noun.

1. My mom **hung** a bird feeder outside the kitchen **window**.

2. Sometimes we **see** five or six **hummingbirds** in one day.

3. Yesterday, we saw a **beautiful** hummingbird with a bright green **head**.

Underline each proper noun in these sentences. Circle each plural noun.

4. Wild canaries live on the Canary Islands off the coast of Africa.

5. Wild canaries can sing.

6. Their songs are not as beautiful as the songs of tame canaries.

7. One kind of canary from Belgium has such a long neck that its head droops.

8. Canaries have been used to detect poison gases in coal mines.

Pronouns

Circle each possessive pronoun in these sentences.

9. Denise gave her grandmother a pet bird for Christmas.

10. The bird has a red beak and yellow feathers on its head.

Circle each interrogative pronoun. Draw a line under each personal pronoun.

11. What does the bird eat?

12. It eats nuts and seeds.

13. Who helped Denise pick out the bird?

14. Roger and I helped Denise choose the perfect bird.

Adjectives, Adverbs, and Prepositions

Decide whether each boldfaced word is an adjective, an adverb, or a preposition. Write *adj., adv.,* or *prep.* after each sentence.

15. Here are some **interesting** facts about birds. _____

16. The tailorbird sews leaves together **skillfully** to make a nest. _____

17. A frigatebird has a sac **under** its beak. _____

18. A 200-pound person could stand **on** an ostrich egg. _____

Verbs

Write *A* above each action verb and *L* above each linking verb.

19. Ostrich eggs are much bigger than chicken eggs.

20. The bee hummingbird is only two inches long.

21. This bird lives in Cuba.

Write *H* above each helping verb and *M* above each main verb.

22. A ten-week-old South American hoatzin chick can fly.

23. Before then, it can swim under water.

Conjunctions

Pick a conjunction in ( ) to join each pair of sentences. Write the new sentence.

24. Pink flamingos live in marshy areas. They eat shellfish. (and/but/or) _____

   _____

25. Most flamingos live for 15 to 20 years in the wild. They may survive even longer in

   captivity. (and/but/or) _____

   _____

Name _____

Beasts & Critters

FAMILY LEARNING OPPORTUNITIES

In Unit 2 of *G.U.M.* we are learning about different parts of speech. For example, we're learning that nouns name people, places, and things. The activities on this page give extra practice with some of the concepts we're learning. You can help your child by choosing one or more of these activities to complete with your child at home.

How-To (Adjectives and Adverbs)

Ask your child to watch as you do some task, such as sewing on a button, measuring ingredients for pancake batter, or raking leaves. Encourage him or her to take notes about the way you do the task.

Then work with your child to rewrite the notes as a list of how-to instructions. Help your child use adjectives (**long** piece of thread) and adverbs (He **carefully** threads) to make the instructions more exact.

| Example | He cuts a **long** piece of thread. He **carefully** threads the needle. |

Guess Who? (Personal and Possessive Pronouns)

Ask your child to think of a person you both know. Then have your child use personal and possessive pronouns to write three clues about the mystery person.

| Example | **I** spend the night at **her** house sometimes. **She** has red hair. **Her** dog is named Georgette. |

Then try to guess the name of the secret person. After you have guessed, read the clues again and underline personal and possessive pronouns. Personal pronouns include *I, me, you, we, us, he, him, she, her, they, them,* and *it.* Possessive pronouns include *my, your, his, her, its, their,* and *our.*

Twenty Questions (Nouns)

This guessing game can be played by two to eight people. One person thinks of a person, place, or thing but keeps it a secret. The other players try to guess what word the person is thinking of by asking questions that can be answered "yes" or "no." Guessers can ask a total of twenty questions before the mystery noun is revealed.

Who's Who? (Proper Nouns)

Ask your child to list the proper names of eight persons, places, or things. Then ask your child to write the appropriate common noun next to each proper noun.

Example
Mr. Hoy—math teacher
Betty McCullough—grandmother

Then have your child scramble the two lists and give them to a family member to match.

Gimme the Facts! (Pronouns That Ask Questions)

Read a short newspaper article with your child. Work together to write five questions that begin with *who, what,* or *which.* (The answers to the questions should be in the news article.) Then ask your child to give the article and the list of questions to you or another family member to answer.

Crossword Puzzle (Singular and Plural Nouns)

Use the clues to complete the crossword puzzle. Each answer is a plural noun.

Across

3. Plural of *tax*
4. When you are introduced to someone, you might shake __.
7. On summer evenings, some people sit out on their __ .
8. Five __ make thirty.

Down

1. Plural of *wish*
2. One candy, many __
5. One arch, many __
6. The pony ran off to join the other __.

Name _____

Beasts & Critters

Read and Discover

"Get out **your** warm clothes," the weather announcer said. "**You're** going to need them."

Underline the boldfaced word that means "you are." Circle the boldfaced word that shows ownership.

The words *your* and *you're* sound the same, but they have different spellings and meanings. *Your* is a possessive pronoun. It means "something that belongs to you." *You're* is a contraction made from the words "you are."

See Handbook Sections 16, 24, and 28

Part 1

Circle the word in ( ) that completes each sentence correctly. (1–10)

"(Your/You're) in for a big surprise this morning," said the weather announcer. "Look out (your/you're) window. You'll see four feet of fresh snow in (your/you're) yard. Find (your/you're) snow shovel and clear the driveway. All schools have been closed due to the snow. (Your/You're) going to have plenty of time to relax today."

Mrs. Kim saw her daughter Yung-Min scooting down the hall. "Where do you think (your/you're) going?" Mrs. Kim called.

"I'm going to build a snowman!" Yung-Min answered.

"(Your/You're) not going anywhere until you put on (your/you're) warm jacket."

"Okay," said Yung-Min. "Then may I use (your/you're) garden shovel to dig in the snow?" she asked.

"Yes, if (your/you're) careful with it," answered Mrs. Kim.

Part 2 ✎

Write *your* or *you're* to complete each sentence correctly. Remember to capitalize a word that begins a sentence.

11. "_____ not going to believe this, but about 89 inches of snow fall each winter in Rochester, New York," said Toby.

12. Denise asked, "Does _____ book describe snow crystals?"

13. "Yes, but _____ going to need a microscope to see how beautiful each crystal is," said Toby.

14. "_____ right," said Denise, peering through the microscope.

15. "The snowflakes _____ looking at are called *platelike* snow crystals."

16. "The crystals under _____ microscope look like stars, but other snowflakes look like long needles."

Part 3 ✎

Use the clues to complete the puzzle. Give each apostrophe its own space in the puzzle.

Across
2. Takes the place of missing letters in a contraction
3. __ going to have fun.
4. Two words made into one

Down
1. Are you sure __ listening?
3. Let's go in __ car.

Name _____

The World Outside

Read and Discover

Those scientists over **there** are meteorologists. **They're** trained to predict the weather. People rely on **their** weather reports.

| belonging to them | | in that place | | they are |

Draw a line from each boldfaced word to the box that shows its meaning.

The words *their, there,* and *they're* sound alike, but they have different spellings and meanings. *Their* is a possessive pronoun that means "something that belongs to them." *There* is an adverb that means "in that place." *They're* is a contraction made from two words. It means "they are."

See Handbook Sections 24, 26, and 28

Part 1

Circle the word in ( ) that completes each sentence. (1–7)

"Meteorologists use weather balloons to gather (their/there) information," explained our science teacher. "They send (their/there) balloons into the sky. While the balloons are up (there/their), they gather information about wind, clouds, rain, and snow."

She explained that the balloons carry instruments called *radiosondes.* (Their/They're) able to measure moisture and wind. The radiosondes send (there/their) information to radio transmitters on the ground.

"How do meteorologists get the radiosondes down once they send them up (there/they're)?" I asked.

Weather balloons gather information about the weather.

"Weather balloons are filled with helium or hydrogen," the teacher said. "(They're/Their) designed to burst when they get to about 90,000 feet. Radiosondes have parachutes attached to them. When the balloon bursts, the radiosondes float to the ground."

Part 2

Write *their*, *there*, or *they're* below. Remember to capitalize a word that begins a sentence.

8. A radiosonde landed over _____ .

9. Mr. and Mrs. Lopez found it in _____ backyard.

10. Now _____ waiting for two scientists to pick it up.

11. The scientists will arrive soon. _____ anxious to see the information

   collected by the radiosonde.

12. Mrs. Lopez was excited to see radiosondes up close. "_____ amazing

   instruments!" she exclaimed.

13. "But why did they land right _____ in my garden?" Mr. Lopez asked.

14. "As soon as the meteorologists come and get _____ equipment, I'll

   help you replant your tulips," Mrs. Lopez replied.

Part 3

Write *their*, *there*, or *they're* to complete each clue. Then solve the riddle.

15. _____ home is in the sky.

16. _____ made of tiny water droplets or ice crystals in the air.

17. _____ shapes often resemble animals.

18. People enjoy lying on _____ backs and watching them pass overhead.

19. _____ a welcome sight when the weather has been hot and dry.

20. Look up _____! I see some now!

What are they? They're ____ ____ ____ ____ ____ ____.

Name _____

The **World** Outside

Read and Discover

A hurricane is a powerful storm. **Its** name comes from a Carib Indian word that means "big wind." If you live in an area where there are hurricanes, **it's** important to be prepared for them. Circle the boldfaced word that means "it is." Underline the boldfaced word that means "belonging to it."

The words *its* and *it's* sound the same, but they have different spellings and meanings. *Its* is a possessive pronoun that means "belonging to it." *It's* is a contraction made from two words and means "it is."

See Handbook Sections 16, 24, and 28

Part 1

Circle the word in ( ) that correctly completes each sentence. (1–9)

A hurricane forms over an ocean. (It's/Its) made up of two parts. The eye of a hurricane is (it's/its) center. (It's/Its) a calm, still area about 20 miles across. Wall clouds surround the eye. A hurricane's strong winds and rain occur in the wall clouds.

(It's/Its) important for weather forecasters to know when a hurricane is coming. Hurricane winds can blow up to 150 miles per hour. A hurricane can leave great damage in (it's/its) path. (It's/Its) also common for hurricanes to produce huge waves. Forecasters carefully watch areas in the ocean where hurricanes form. When they

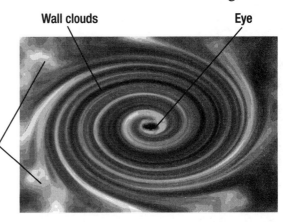

Wall clouds   Eye

Rain clouds

It's calm inside the hurricane's eye.

notice a hurricane forming, they use data to predict (it's/its) strength. They also predict when and where (it's/its) likely to strike. Weather forecasters warn people of the approaching hurricane. People who live in (it's/its) path can then take shelter.

The World Outside

Part 2

Write *its* or *it's* to complete each sentence correctly. Remember to capitalize a word if it begins a sentence.

10. _____ hurricane season from June to November in the United States.

11. Usually about six hurricanes happen in the world's northern oceans each year, but

    _____ not unusual for more to occur.

12. In 1969 Hurricane Camille left terrible destruction in _____ path.

13. _____ winds knocked down buildings and uprooted trees.

14. In the Americas this kind of storm is called a *hurricane,* but in the Indian Ocean

    _____ called a *cyclone.*

15. In parts of the Pacific Ocean _____ called a *typhoon.*

16. _____ important to take shelter in a hurricane!

Part 3

Imagine you are a TV weather announcer. Write a description of the weather in your community today. Use *its* and *it's* correctly.

_____

_____

_____

_____

_____

Name _____

The World Outside

Read and Discover

It **was** cold last winter. Many days **were** below freezing.

Is the subject of the first sentence singular or plural?

_____ Which verb is used in the first sentence? _____

Is the subject of the second sentence singular or plural?

_____ Which verb is used in the second sentence? _____

The linking verb *be* does not show action. It tells what someone or something is or was like. The verb *be* has different forms when it is used with singular subjects and plural subjects. The subject and its verb **must agree.**

📢 **Remember to use this information when you speak, too.**

Present Tense	Past Tense
I *am* cold.	Yesterday the weather *was* chilly.
We *are* cold.	Even the birds *were* cold.

Remember to use *has* or *have* with the verb *been.*

He *has been* cold for weeks. They *have been* cold before.

See Handbook Sections 17 and 27

Part 1 ✏️

Circle the word in ( ) that completes each sentence.

1. The atmosphere (is/are) the air around Earth.

2. The atmosphere (is/are) about 1,000 miles high.

3. Four different layers of air (is/are) in the atmosphere.

4. The lowest layer of air (is/are) the troposphere.

5. Most of Earth's weather systems (is/are) in this low layer.

6. People (has/have) been interested in weather for centuries.

7. Galileo (was/were) one of the first weather scientists.

8. The thermometer (was/were) his invention.

9. Thermometers (has/have) been widely used for centuries.

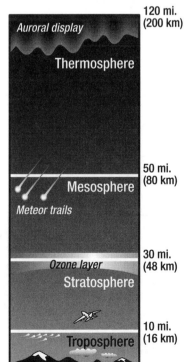

The World Outside

Part 2

Write a word from the word bank to complete each sentence.

is	are	was	were	been

10. Some ancient peoples believed that the stars _____ responsible for the

    weather.

11. The ancient people of Scandinavia believed that a god named Thor _____

    responsible for thunder.

12. Scientists now know that wind, moisture, and temperature _____ the

    causes of weather.

13. Wind _____ probably the most important element.

14. Weather balloons and radar have _____ helpful tools for meteorologists.

15. Meteorologists' weather reports _____ important in our daily lives.

Part 3

Write two or three sentences about the layers of air that surround Earth. The picture
on page 65 can help you. Use a form of the verb *be* in each sentence.

_____

_____

_____

_____

_____

Name _____

The World Outside

Read and Discover

I cannot see **well** in this hot desert sun! I need a **good** hat to shade my eyes.

Circle the boldfaced word that describes a noun. Underline the boldfaced word that describes a verb.

> *Good* is an adjective that describes a noun. *Well* is an adverb that describes a verb. **Remember to use this information when you speak, too.**
>
> **See Handbook Section 27**

Part 1

Decide whether the word in ( ) will describe a noun or a verb. Then circle *good* or *well* to complete each sentence correctly. (1–9)

Death Valley is (good/well) known for its hot climate. The temperature can reach 125°F in summer! People do not do (good/well) in that kind of heat. April is a (good/well) month to visit Death Valley.

We planned (good/well) for our trip to Death Valley. We brought (good/well) hiking boots, plenty of food, and fresh water.

We also visited Mount Whitney, one of the highest mountains in the United States. The weather was (good/well) when we hiked to the top of Mount Whitney. We climbed more than 14,000 feet! I couldn't breathe (good/well) at the top because the air was thin.

Death Valley, California, is the hottest place in the Western Hemisphere.

After the hike we cooked a (good/well) dinner at our campground. I slept (good/well) that night!

Part 2

The sentences below give safety tips for camping. Rewrite each sentence to include *good* or *well*.

10. Bring a compass. _____

11. Study your maps. _____

12. Wear boots. _____

13. Carry a backpack. _____

14. Be sure to eat. _____

15. Sleep at night. _____

16. Clean your campsite. _____

Part 3

Write three more survival tips for a hot climate. You may use some of the words in the word bank. Use *good* and *well* correctly.

hat	canteen	tent	rest	protect	drink

17. _____

_____

18. _____

_____

19. _____

_____

Name _____

The World Outside

Read and Discover

"Thunder and lightning **don't** scare me," said Jeremy. "Rain **doesn't** scare me either."

Which boldfaced verb is used with a singular subject? _____

Which boldfaced verb is used with a plural subject? _____

The negative forms of the verb *do* are **doesn't** and **don't**. *Doesn't* means "does not." Use *doesn't* with a singular subject and with the pronouns *he*, *she*, and *it*. *Don't* means "do not." Use *don't* with a plural subject and with the pronouns *I*, *you*, *we*, and *they*. **Remember to use this information when you speak, too.**

See Handbook Sections 22, 24, and 27

Part 1

Underline the word in ( ) that belongs in each sentence. (1–9)

Sue gave a report about rainbows. "Most rainbows appear after a rainstorm. Rainbows (don't/doesn't) form unless sunlight shines through raindrops. Sunlight is made of different colors, but we (don't/doesn't) usually see them. When sunlight passes through raindrops, the light is bent so that the colors can be seen." Sue told us that the light from the moon can make rainbows, too, but we (don't/doesn't) usually see these because they are so faint.

Sue said, "Double rainbows (don't/doesn't) occur often. I (don't/doesn't) think I have ever seen one. Double rainbows happen when the sun shines on a shower that is moving away."

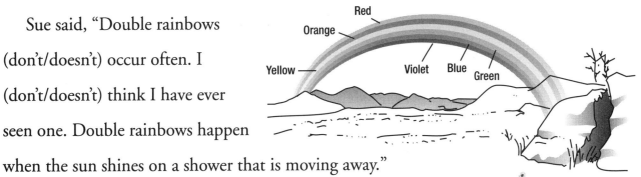

Red
Orange
Yellow
Violet   Blue   Green

Sue explained that a rainbow is made up of six colors. "We usually (don't/doesn't) see all six," she said, "because the colors blend. A rainbow (don't/doesn't) always stretch all the way across the sky. Sometimes it (don't/doesn't) look very bright. An old story says that there is a pot of gold at the end of every rainbow. I (don't/doesn't) believe this is true."

Part 2

Circle the subject of each sentence. Then write *doesn't* or *don't* to complete each sentence correctly. Remember to capitalize the first word in a sentence.

10. I _____ see the rainbow.

11. Bill _____ see it either.

12. We _____ know where to look.

13. I _____ have my field glasses.

14. He hopes it _____ rain now.

15. I _____ have my raincoat.

16. Naomi _____ have her umbrella, either.

17. A rainbow _____ last for long.

18. _____ you see the colors in the sky?

Part 3

Draw and color a double rainbow below. Use the color labels on page 69 to help you. Then write a sentence describing your rainbow. Use *don't* and *doesn't* correctly.

_____

_____

Name _____

Read and Discover

We're expecting **a** hailstorm today. Do you have **an** umbrella? Circle the boldfaced word that comes before the word beginning with a consonant sound.

A, an, and *the* are special adjectives called articles. Use *a* in front of a noun or a word that begins with a consonant sound. Use *an* in front of a noun or a word that begins with a vowel sound. Use *a* and *an* when talking about any person, place, or thing. Use *the* when talking about a specific person, place, or thing. **Remember to use this information when you speak, too.**

See Handbook Section 27

Part 1

Circle the word in ( ) to complete each sentence correctly.

1. A hailstone is (a/an/the) ball of ice.

2. A hailstone's construction is similar to (a/an/the) onion's.

3. (A/An/The) hailstone has many layers, or shells, of ice.

4. A hailstone can be as small as (a/an/the) pea.

5. It can be as large as (a/an/the) apple.

6. (A/An/The) largest hailstone ever found landed during a rainstorm in Coffeyville, Kansas, in 1970.

The largest hailstone ever recorded was almost six inches tall.

7. At 17 inches around, (a/an/the) hailstone was a monster!

8. Large hailstones like that pose (a/an/the) danger to people, crops, and plants.

9. Large hailstones can dent (a/an/the) automobile's roof.

10. Luckily, most hailstones are less than (a/an/the) inch in size.

The World Outside

Part 2

Write *a*, *an*, or *the* to complete each sentence correctly. Remember to capitalize the first word in a sentence.

11. Hail forms in _____ cold cloud.

12. A hailstone begins as _____ tiny drop of frozen water.

13. _____ updraft of air keeps the hailstone swirling through the cloud.

14. It collects moisture as it moves, and _____ shell of ice forms around it.

15. Large hailstones have swirled inside the cloud for _____ long period of time.

16. Hailstones fall at about 22 miles _____ hour.

Part 3

Pretend you are a reporter covering a storm of giant hailstones. Write about what you see. Use some of the words in the word bank. Make sure to use *a*, *an*, and *the* correctly.

inches	hour	ouch	pound	umbrella	helmets

_____

_____

_____

_____

_____

_____

_____

Name _____

Read and Discover

Whose newspaper is this?
Who's going to need the weather report?
Circle the boldfaced word that means "who is." Underline the boldfaced word that shows ownership.

> *Whose* and *who's* sound the same, but they have different spellings and meanings. *Whose* is a possessive pronoun. It shows ownership. *Who's* is a contraction made from two words. It means "who is." Both *whose* and *who's* can be used to ask questions.

See Handbook Sections 7, 24, and 28

Part 1

Underline the word in ( ) that fits in each sentence.

1. (Whose/Who's) satellite is that, orbiting Earth?

2. My uncle, (whose/who's) an astronomer, says it's a United States weather satellite.

3. (Whose/Who's) telescope is this?

4. (Whose/Who's) going to set up the telescope?

5. (Whose/Who's) job is it to collect the information the satellite beams to Earth?

6. The scientist (whose/who's) talking on the telephone is the one who collects the information.

Photos taken by weather satellites are seen on TV news programs.

7. (Whose/Who's) interested in the information?

8. Weather reports help people (whose/who's) work is affected by the weather.

9. (Whose/Who's) job is it to warn people of dangerous storms?

10. The National Weather Service, (whose/who's) headquarters is near Washington, D.C., does this job.

The World Outside

Part 2

Write *whose* or *who's* to complete each sentence correctly. Remember to capitalize the first word in a sentence.

11. _____ the inventor of the raincoat? A Scottish chemist named Charles

Macintosh invented it in 1823.

12. _____ galoshes are these?

13. _____ umbrella is dripping in the hallway?

14. _____ going outside with me?

15. Will the person _____ overcoat this is please hang it up?

Part 3

Find seven nouns hidden in the puzzle. Then write two questions about the words you find. Use *whose* in one question and *who's* in the other.

Z	X	D	G	S	K	M	C	J	R
B	U	W	T	H	Q	B	H	V	N
X	M	F	A	J	L	P	C	M	T
C	B	V	L	R	P	B	D	D	H
N	R	A	I	N	C	O	A	T	U
T	E	L	E	V	I	S	I	O	N
P	L	Q	N	R	T	X	G	Y	D
H	L	M	V	B	G	F	L	C	E
S	A	T	E	L	L	I	T	E	R
J	S	K	S	V	G	Z	W	K	T

_____

_____

_____

Name _____

The World Outside

Read and Discover

Tornadoes are caused by **two** movements of air. Cold air from Canada blows northwest **to** southeast. Warm air from Mexico blows north. Storms build where these air masses meet. Most tornadoes are in Kansas and Oklahoma. They occur in Texas, **too**.

Circle the boldfaced word that means "also." Underline the boldfaced word that means "toward." Draw a box around the boldfaced word that means "one plus one."

Two, too, and *to* sound the same, but they have different spellings and meanings. *Two* is a number. *Too* means "also" or "more than enough." *To* often means "toward."

See Handbook Section 28

Part 1

Circle the word in ( ) that completes each sentence. (1–8)

Scientists from the National Severe Storms Laboratory in Norman, Oklahoma, study tornadoes. Students and teachers from the University of Oklahoma study tornadoes, (two/too/to). Sometimes these (two/too/to) groups work together.

Tornado season in Oklahoma lasts for about (two/too/to) months. During that time, tornado chasers travel (two/too/to) places where they think tornadoes will strike. They take a special device called TOTO with them. TOTO is named after Dorothy's dog in the movie *The Wizard of Oz.* TOTO is a strong metal barrel. It is designed (two/too/to) be picked up by tornadoes. It carries instruments that measure the winds inside a tornado.

About 850 tornadoes twirl across the U.S. every year.

The tornado chasers' work is exciting, but it's dangerous, (two/too/to). They must try (two/too/to) put TOTO in a tornado's path. Then they must hurry (two/too/to) safety.

The World Outside

Part 2

Write *two*, *too*, or *to* on the lines to complete the sentences. Remember to capitalize a word that begins a sentence.

9. I see _____ funnel-shaped clouds!

10. I see a third cloud _____ the north!

11. Let's go down _____ the storm cellar.

12. Bring _____ flashlights with you.

13. Bring a radio and batteries, _____.

14. You can't be _____ prepared for a tornado.

15. _____ tornadoes touched down last week.

16. One touched down yesterday, _____.

17. Let's listen _____ the weather report.

Part 3

Write an answer for each clue. Then use the circled letters to answer the riddle.

18. Dorothy's dog   ◯ __ __ __

19. what rain, wind, and snow are   ◯ __ __ __ __ __

20. electric bolt in the sky   __ __ __ __ __ __ ◯ __ __

21. a state south of Oklahoma   __ __ __ ◯ __

22. a funnel cloud   ◯ __ __ __ __ __ __

23. a clap of   __ __ __ __ __ ◯ ◯ __

What is another name for a tornado?   __ __ __ __ __ __

Name _____

Read and Discover

A tornado can pick up heavy objects and **throw** them great distances. Tornadoes have **thrown** trains, trailers, and trees. Circle the form of the verb *throw* that is used with *have*.

Throw and *catch* are irregular verbs. You cannot make the past tense of these verbs by adding *-ed*. These verbs have different forms.
Remember to use this information when you speak, too.

Present	Past	With *have, has,* or *had*
throw(s)	threw	thrown
catch(es)	caught	caught

See Handbook Section 17

Part 1

Circle the verb in ( ) that belongs in each sentence.

1. The tornado (catched/caught) us by surprise.

2. When we heard its low roar, we (throwed/threw) flashlights and matches into a box.

3. "(Threw/Throw) me the radio!" I shouted.

4. I (catched/caught) the radio in one hand and grabbed some batteries with the other.

5. Dad (threw/throwed) open the door to the storm cellar.

6. Dad leaped down first, and he (catched/caught) me as I jumped to safety.

7. We listened to the tornado (threw/throw) things around above ground, and when it was over we checked the damage.

8. The tornado had (threw/thrown) a car onto the roof of a house!

9. The tornado's winds had (threw/thrown) debris everywhere.

10. Never let a tornado (caught/catch) you above ground!

The World Outside

Part 2

Use the correct form of *throw* or *catch* to complete the answer to each question.

11. Did the storm <u>catch</u> you by surprise?

    Yes, _____.

12. Did you <u>throw</u> away your old umbrella?

    Yes, _____.

13. Can a person <u>catch</u> a tornado?

    No, _____.

14. Have tornadoes <u>thrown</u> cars onto roofs?

    Yes, _____.

15. Have you ever <u>caught</u> a tornado's motion on film?

    Yes, _____.

Part 3

Use the clues to complete the puzzle with forms of *throw* or *catch*.

Across
2. Rosario's dog Spot can __ Frisbees.
4. Rosario once __ his Frisbee over a fence, and Spot still got it!
5. Once Rosario has __ the Frisbee, Spot jumps for it.

Down
1. Spot __ most of Rosario's throws today.
3. Spot could have __ more.
4. Tomorrow he'll catch every Frisbee Rosario __.

Name _____

The World Outside

Proofreading Others' Writing

Read this report about lightning. Find the mistakes. Use the proofreading marks below to show how each mistake should be fixed.

Proofreading Marks

Mark	Means	Example
℘	take away	Lightning comes before before thunder.
∧	add	Lightning before thunder.
≡	make into a capital letter	lightning comes before thunder.
/	make into a lowercase letter	Lightning comes before Thunder.
⊙	add a period	Lightning comes before thunder
sp	fix spelling	Litning comes before thunder.

Lightning

Lightning is a huge electrical spark that flashes in the sky Their are different kinds of lightning. Most of the lightning we see happens between the clouds and the earth. This is called *cloud-to-earth* lightning. Lightening can also flash from one cloud two another. Your likely to see this kind of lightning from a airplane. *Intracloud* lightning flashes within a single cloud. We cannot see intracloud lighting very good from the ground.

Have you ever wondered how long a bolt of lightning is? The shortest lightning bolts is about 300 feet long. These occur in mountainous places where the clouds are very low. In flat regions where the clouds are high, lightning bolts are usually five too nine miles long.

How wide is a lightning bolt? Its not as wide as you would think. Some experts believe that the core of an lightning bolt is only a half inch wide. The core may be surrounded by a glowing band of light that is 10–20 feet across. You can see the length of a lightning bolt when it is catched on film.

Proofreading Your Own Writing

You can use the list below to help you find and fix mistakes in your own writing. Write the titles of your own stories or reports in the blanks on top of the chart. Then use the questions to check your work. Make a check mark (✓) in each box after you have checked that item.

Titles

Proofreading Checklist for Unit 3

Does each sentence have a subject and a predicate?				
Have I used words that sound the same, but have different spellings, correctly?				
Have I used the words *don't, doesn't, well, good, a, an,* and *the* correctly?				
Have I used the correct past-tense forms of irregular verbs?				
Have I used forms of *be* correctly?				

Also Remember . . .

Does each sentence begin with a capital letter?				
Does each sentence end with the right mark?				
Have I spelled each word correctly?				
Have I used commas correctly?				

Your Own List

Use this space to write your own list of things to check in your writing.

Name _____

Usage

Underline a word in ( ) to complete each sentence correctly.

1. From spring until fall, (a/an) strong wind called a *monsoon* blows over India.

2. Monsoons blow over Pakistan and Bangladesh, (to/too).

3. The rain clouds they bring are (a/an) welcome sight to farmers.

4. (Their/They're) fields remain cracked and dry until the monsoons come.

5. The storms bring heavy rains (to/too) the cities and towns of India.

6. Floods can damage streets, buildings, and railways (their/there).

7. There are (too/two) ways to look at the monsoons.

8. (They're/Their) good for farmers, but they cause hardship and damage, too.

9. A volcano in Mexico called *El Chichón* (thrown/threw) tons of ash into the air when it exploded.

10. People who lived in the area were (catched/caught) by surprise.

11. There (had/have) been a rumbling noise coming from the volcano for months.

12. Some people (were/was) injured by the falling rocks and ash.

13. A huge cloud of ash (were/was) sent into the atmosphere.

14. This cloud (is/are) a worry to some scientists.

More Usage

Choose a word in ( ) and write it on the line to complete the sentence correctly.

15. If you were a spiny-tailed lizard, _____ home would be

the Sahara desert. (you're/your)

16. The desert _____ get much rain. (doesn't/don't)

17. The spiny lizard _____ need much water. (doesn't/don't)

18. It has adapted well to _____ hot, dry home. (its/it's)

19. At night, _____ cool in the desert. (it's/its)

20. The weather in a tropical rain forest is _____ for plants

that need a lot of water. (good/well)

21. These plants grow _____ because at least 80 inches of

rain fall each year in the rain forest. (good/well)

Write *Whose* or *Who's* on the lines to complete the sentences.

22. _____ your local weather forecaster? Our local weather

forecaster is Maggie McCloud.

23. _____ home is in an area where there is very little rain?

My home is in a desert where there is very little rain.

24. _____ going to listen to the radio so we know what to

wear when we go outside? Jeremy will listen and tell us what to wear.

25. _____ raincoat is that? It belongs to me.

Name _____

The World Outside

FAMILY LEARNING OPPORTUNITIES

In Unit 3 of *G.U.M.* we are learning how to use words that can be confusing, such as *its* and *it's* and *their* and *there*. The activities on these pages give extra practice with some of the concepts we're learning. You can help your child understand some of the concepts he or she is learning in school by choosing one or more activities to complete with your child at home.

Weather Forecast (*Its* and *It's; Your* and *You're*)

With your child, read the weather reports in your local newspaper for about a week. Work together to write an illustrated forecast for each day. Post the forecast at home or in your workplace. Try to use these words in your forecast: *its, it's, you're, your.*

Sam's Two-Day Outlook

It's going to be sunny but chilly, so don't forget your overcoat.

You're going to need an extra sweater today because winter is on its way.

Word Search (*Two, Too, To; Good* and *Well;* Irregular Verbs: *Throw* and *Catch*)

There are ten words hidden in the puzzle. Work with your child to see who is the first to find them all. Then ask your child to use each word in a sentence.

T	O	O	M	P	X	P	V	R	C	P
W	L	P	K	G	O	O	D	W	S	H
O	L	X	Q	M	Z	Q	D	X	Z	P
X	C	A	T	C	H	J	W	K	T	Y
N	A	X	H	B	D	N	E	Q	H	K
P	U	F	R	S	Q	P	L	I	R	M
F	G	U	E	Z	N	N	L	X	O	W
K	H	X	W	T	T	H	R	O	W	N
H	T	N	P	S	S	Q	T	O	L	V

Cloud Watch (Forms of *Be*)

Watch cloud formations with your child and work together to write descriptions of the most unusual clouds you see. Use forms of the verb *be* (*is, are, was, were, been*) in your description.

Examples

Tuesday: The clouds **are** puffy and white. One cloud **is** the shape of an elephant.
Wednesday: At sunrise the clouds **were** pink and gold. In the afternoon they **were** thin and wispy. Now they **are** dark and stormy.

Adverb Search (Irregular Verbs: *Throw* and *Catch*)

Some verbs do not add *-ed* in the past tense. These verbs are irregular.

Example

The past tense of **throw** is **threw**.

With your child, hunt for other irregular verbs in a newspaper, magazine, or comic book. First, have your child find the verb in a sentence. Then use the verb in a sentence about the present and another sentence about the past.

Example

Throw the ball now.
I already **threw** the ball.

Try to find and list as many irregular verbs as you can. Some irregular verbs are *sleep/slept, catch/caught,* and *make/made*.

Guessing Game (*Doesn't* and *Don't*)

Follow these steps with your child to create a guessing game your whole family can play:

1. Cut thick paper into six 3" x 5" cards. (Or use index cards.) Give each team of two players three cards.
2. Team members should write five or six clues to the identity of one animal on each card. Some of the clues should include the word *doesn't* or *don't*.
3. Ask teams to exchange cards, read the clues, and name the animal.

Example

- It has wings, but it **doesn't** fly.
- You **don't** find it in warm places.
- It **doesn't** live alone.
- It is black and white.
- It likes ice and snow.

You might enjoy making up additional categories, such as *clothing* or *food*.

Name _____

The World Outside

Read and Discover

Our class is studying state histories. This week, **we** are learning about Texas.

Look at the boldfaced word. Circle the underlined words it takes the place of. Are these underlined words the subject of the sentence or the object of the verb? _____

> A **subject pronoun** takes the place of one or more nouns in the subject of a sentence. *I, you, he, she,* and *it* are singular subject pronouns. *We, you,* and *they* are plural subject pronouns.
>
> **See Handbook Section 16**

Part 1

Underline the six subject pronouns in these paragraphs. (1–6)

Our history teacher told us that thousands of Native Americans lived in the Texas area long ago. She said that many of these Native Americans were farmers.

In the early 1500s people from Spain began to explore the Texas region. They were looking for gold. In 1519 a man from Spain named Alonso Álvarez de Piñeda explored the Gulf Coast. He drew a map of the coastal region of Texas. Piñeda and his companions were among the first Europeans to travel there.

Texas was part of Spanish territory until 1821. Then it became part of the Empire of Mexico. Many individuals from the eastern and southern United States settled there during the 1820s. A number of these settlers were not pleased with how Texas was being governed. They began to fight for independence from Mexico in 1835. Eventually they won their independence.

Spain established many missions throughout Texas in the 1700s.

Looking Back

Part 2 ✏️

Choose a subject pronoun from the word bank that can take the place of the boldfaced word or words in each sentence. Rewrite the sentence using that pronoun. You can use the same pronoun more than once.

It	You	They	She	We	He

7. **Jo and I** saw a film about the Texans' dramatic defense of the Alamo in 1836.

   _____

   _____

8. **The small Texas army** defeated the Mexican Army at San Jacinto in that year.

   _____

   _____

9. **Sam Houston** was elected president of the new Republic of Texas. _____

   _____

10. **The Republic of Texas** became a state in 1845. _____

   _____

Part 3 ✏️

Decide which of these Texas attractions you would like to visit. Write one sentence explaining why you would like to go there. Use subject pronouns in your answer.

Six Flags over Texas is an amusement park based on Texas history.
The Alamo is the site of one of the most famous battles in American history.

_____

_____

_____

Name _____

Read and Discover

We learn about the California Gold Rush through different sources. Many stories have been passed down to **us** in diaries.

Which boldfaced pronoun is the subject of a sentence? _____

Which boldfaced pronoun is the object of a sentence? _____

> An **object pronoun** takes the place of one or more nouns. Object pronouns follow action verbs or prepositions, words such as *to, at, for, of,* and *with*. Singular object pronouns are *me, you, him, her,* and *it*. Plural object pronouns are *us, you,* and *them*.
>
> See Handbook Section 16

Part 1

Circle the object pronouns in the sentences below. Try to find all ten. **(1–10)**

James W. Marshall found a gold nugget in Coloma, California, in 1848. The find made him famous. The next year, thousands of people went to California. They hoped that gold would make them rich.

Sarah Royce traveled to California during the Gold Rush of 1849. My history teacher told me about her. Sarah Royce kept a diary. In it, she wrote about the journey west. This diary tells us what life was like in California long ago.

Many people traveled in covered wagons on their way west.

Sarah Royce's husband bought a covered wagon. The couple traveled across America, bringing their baby girl with them. The Royces lost the trail in the desert. They found it again just before they ran out of food and water. They arrived at the high, snowy Sierra Nevada mountains just before winter. They crossed them before the winter storms began. Does this journey sound easy to you?

Part 2

Complete each sentence with an object pronoun from the word bank.

you	us	her	me	it	him	them

11. The Royces finally reached California. They found a mining camp, and the people there said, "Come join _____."

12. They couldn't build a house, but a tent protected _____ from rain and snow.

13. The decorations they added to the tent made _____ more pleasant.

14. Sarah Royce's husband opened a store. Sarah helped _____.

15. This work was new for _____, and Sarah had to learn new skills.

16. Miners paid gold dust to _____ for supplies.

17. If you'd like, I'll lend my copy of Sarah Royce's diary to _____.

18. Please give the book back to _____ when you're done.

Part 3

Find seven object pronouns in the word search. Then write two sentences about a journey you would like to make. Use at least one object pronoun.

K	V	I	T	U	W
Z	Y	O	U	L	H
Y	I	E	K	T	I
H	E	R	X	H	M
S	F	T	U	E	A
M	E	D	S	M	O

19. _____

_____

20. _____

_____

Looking Back

Read and Discover

Jo moved to Montana two years ago and met her cousin Bob for the first time. **He** met **her** at the airport.
Circle the boldfaced pronoun that is the subject of the sentence. Underline the boldfaced pronoun that is the object of the sentence.

Use the pronouns *I, we, he, she,* and *they* as subjects in sentences.
Use the pronouns *me, us, him, her,* and *them* as objects in sentences.
▶ **Remember to use this information when you speak, too.**

See Handbook Section 16

Part 1

Circle the correct word in ( ) to complete each sentence. Label the sentence *S* if the answer is a *subject pronoun* and *O* if the answer is an *object pronoun.*

1. Bob and (I/me) discovered that the name *Montana* comes from a Spanish word meaning "mountainous." ____

2. Mrs. Hoy told Jo and (he/him) that most of Montana was part of the Louisiana Purchase. ____

3. Jo and (me/I) learned that prospectors found gold in Montana in the 1860s. ____

4. Jo and (I/me) learned that Montana became a state in 1889. ____

5. Mrs. Hoy asked Bob and (she/her) to name the first woman ever elected to Congress. ____

6. (He/Him) and Jo both knew that Jeannette Rankin of Montana was elected in 1916. ____

7. Mrs. Hoy told (us/we) that Rankin opposed American involvement in both World War I and World War II. ____

All or part of eleven national forests are located in Montana.

Part 2 ✏️

Choose a pronoun from the word bank to replace each boldfaced word or phrase. Write the pronoun. If the pronoun would be the first word in the sentence, capitalize it.

she	us	him	he	they	her	we	I

8. **Our class** also read about the Native American groups whose traditional homelands are in Montana. _____

9. Jo said, "**Jo** borrowed a library book about peoples of the Northern Plains." _____

10. **Jo and Bob** are writing a report about the Blackfoot people. _____

11. Mrs. Hoy told Jo and **Bob** that the Blackfoot people call the Rocky Mountains "the backbone of the land." _____

12. **Mrs. Hoy** and Jo described how the Blackfoot people hunted buffalo. _____

13. Mrs. Hoy told Bob and **Jo** that in the nineteenth century, thousands of Blackfoot people lived on the plains in Montana and Canada. _____

14. **Bob** read that many Native Americans celebrate North American Indian Days. _____

15. Jo told **our class** that the celebration is held at the Blackfoot Tribal Fairgrounds in Browning, Montana. _____

Part 3 ✏️

Montana's nickname is "The Big Sky Country." Make up a nickname for your state. Write a sentence about why you chose that nickname. Use pronouns correctly.

_____

_____

_____

Name _____

Looking Back

Read and Discover

I **and Jill** are working on a speech about Iowa. ___
Jill and I are working on a speech about Iowa. ___

The librarian helped **Jill and me** find some good books. ___
The librarian helped **me and Jill** find some good books. ___

Put a check next to the sentence in each pair that sounds better.

I is a **subject pronoun**. It can be used as the subject of a sentence. *Me* is an **object pronoun**. It is used after an action verb or a preposition, such as *at, for,* or *with*. When you talk about yourself and another person, always name the other person first. **Remember to use this information when you speak, too.**

See Handbook Sections 16 and 27

Part 1

Circle the correct group of words in ( ) to complete each sentence.

1. The librarian told (me and Jill/Jill and me) that ninety percent of Iowa is farmland.

2. (Jill and I/Jill and me) read that Iowa's soil is some of the richest on Earth.

3. (Jill and I/Jill and me) drew a picture showing the glaciers that covered Iowa thousands of years ago.

4. The librarian told (Jill and me/me and Jill) that the Missouri, the Illinois, and the Iowa peoples once lived in Iowa.

5. (Me and Jill/Jill and I) realized that many states are named after Native American groups.

6. (Jill and I/Jill and me) reported that French traders explored the Iowa area in 1673.

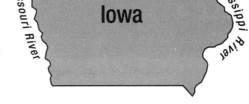

Iowa's eastern border is the Mississippi River. The Missouri River is on the west.

7. (She and I/She and me) also explained that pioneers settled there in the 1830s.

8. (Jill and I/Me and Jill) learned about what life was like for these pioneers.

Looking Back

Part 2

Write words from the word bank to complete each sentence correctly.

Jill	I	me

9. _____ and _____ answered questions about Iowa after our speech.

10. Our teacher asked _____ and _____ to name the first president born west of the Mississippi River.

11. _____ and _____ both knew that Herbert Hoover was born in Iowa.

12. Next, Adam asked _____ and _____ when Iowa became a state.

13. "Iowa became a state in 1846," _____ and _____ told the class.

14. Joline asked _____ and _____ why some people call Iowa the "golden buckle of the corn belt."

15. _____ and _____ explained that farmers in Iowa raise more corn than farmers in any other state.

16. Our class gave _____ and _____ a round of applause when we finished.

Part 3

Imagine that you and a friend went to the Iowa State Fair and saw the biggest pig in Iowa. Write two sentences about it using pronouns. Remember to use *I* and *me* correctly.

_____

_____

_____

_____

Name _____

Looking Back

Read and Discover

This here state is Alaska.
This region is where the first Americans lived.
Draw a star by the sentence that is written correctly.

This, that, these, and *those* can be used as **demonstrative adjectives**. *This* and *these* refer to a thing or things close by. Do not use *here* after *this* or *these*. *That* and *those* refer to a thing or things far away. Do not use *there* after *that* or *those*. **Remember to use this information when you speak, too.**

See Handbook Section 15

Part 1

Circle the answer in ( ) that correctly completes each sentence.

1. (This/Those) plane we're boarding will take us across Alaska.

2. (This/This here) pair of binoculars will help you see the land beneath us.

3. Adjust (these/these here) knobs to focus the binoculars.

4. (That/Those) water in the distance is the Bering Strait.

5. (That there/That) land across the Bering Strait is part of Asia.

6. (That/This) book in my hand tells how the first Americans came from Asia.

7. (These here/These) maps show that long ago the Bering Strait was a land bridge.

8. The ancestors of the Inuit people crossed (this/this here) area I'm pointing to on the map to reach North America.

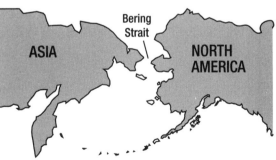

At the Bering Strait, North America and Asia are only 50 miles apart.

9. They hunted fur-bearing mammals like (these/those) seals swimming far below us.

10. The coats of (those there/those) seals are extremely warm.

Looking Back

Part 2

Correct any demonstrative adjectives that have been used incorrectly. Rewrite the sentences correctly.

11. That there flag is the state flag of Alaska. _____

    _____

12. This here plaque I'm reading tells how an Alaskan schoolboy designed the flag.

    _____

    _____

13. When he made the background blue, he was thinking of these here forget-me-not

    flowers growing at our feet. _____

    _____

14. He put gold stars on the flag to represent those stars high in the sky. _____

    _____

Part 3

Draw a flag for your state, town, or school. Write two sentences about your design. Use *this, these, that,* or *those* in your sentences.

_____

_____

_____

_____

_____

Name _____

Looking Back

Read and Discover

NASA <u>launches</u> space shuttles from Kennedy Space Center in Florida. Many tourists <u>visit</u> the center on Merritt Island near Florida's Atlantic coast.

Which underlined verb ends in *s* or *es*? _____

Is the subject of that sentence singular or plural? _____

The **subject** and its **verb must agree**. Add *s* or *es* to a regular verb in the present tense when the subject is a singular noun or *he, she,* or *it*. Do not add *s* or *es* to a regular verb in the present tense when the subject is a plural noun or *I, you, we,* or *they*. ◄ **Remember to use this information when you speak, too.**

See Handbook Section 17

Part 1

Write *S* if the subject is singular and *P* if it is plural. Then circle the verb in ( ) that fits in each sentence.

1. Visitors (watches/watch) shuttle launches at the Kennedy Space Center. ____

2. Florida's rainy weather sometimes (delays/delay) launches. ____

3. However, the sun often (shines/shine) on Florida. ____

4. Tourists (visits/visit) Florida more than almost

   any other state. ____

5. They (enjoys/enjoy) the beauty of the wetlands. ____

6. Many unusual animals (lives/live) in Florida. ____

7. State laws (protects/protect) their habitats. ____

The Kennedy Space Center is home to NASA's space shuttle program.

8. Brown pelicans, herons, and egrets (nests/nest) in Florida's wetlands. ____

9. Still, many tourists (prefers/prefer) the Kennedy Space Center. ____

10. New shuttle missions (makes/make) history there every year. ____

Looking Back

Part 2 ✏️

Write the word in ( ) that will complete each sentence correctly.

11. Many people _____ Dr. Mae Carol Jemison. (admires/admire)

12. Perhaps you already _____ about her many accomplishments.

(know/knows)

13. I _____ her because she was the first African American woman

to travel in space. (respect/respects)

14. On the shuttle she studied how frog eggs _____ in zero gravity.

(grows/grow)

15. Her experiments _____ how gravity affects animals.

(shows/show)

16. Now she _____ to improve health care in Africa. (works/work)

Part 3 ✏️

Imagine that you are an astronaut. Write a few sentences about a mission you would like to go on. Where would you go? What would you do there? Make sure the subject and the verb agree in each sentence.

_____

_____

_____

_____

_____

Name _____

Looking Back

Read and Discover

New York was home to many Native American groups. Underline the simple subject and circle the simple predicate.

Is the subject singular or plural? _____

Am, is, are, was, and were are forms of the verb be. Use am after the pronoun I. Use is or was after a **singular subject**, or after the pronouns he, she, or it. Use are or were after a **plural subject**, or after the pronouns we, you, or they. **Remember to use this information when you speak, too.**

See Handbook Section 17

Part 1

Write *S* next to each sentence with a singular subject. Write *P* next to each sentence with a plural subject. Circle the word in ( ) that fits in each sentence.

1. I (am/is) interested in the history of Native Americans in the state of New York. ___

2. The first known government in New York (was/were) the Iroquois League. ___

3. This league (was/were) a union of Native American nations. ___

4. Men from each nation (was/were) members of the league's Great Council. ___

5. Women (was/were) also important in Iroquois government. ___

6. They (was/were) decision makers. ___
   They decided who would go to the
   Great Council.

7. The United States government (is/are) like the Great Council in some ways. ___

The Iroquois League controlled upper New York from the 1500s until the Revolutionary War.

8. Individual states (is/are) like the nations of the Iroquois League. ___

9. The League (was/were) an inspiration to the writers of the U.S. Constitution. ___

Looking Back

Part 2

Write *is, was, are,* or *were* to complete each sentence correctly.

10. The Dutch people _____ the first European settlers in New York.

11. The Iroquois League members _____ trading partners of the Dutch.

12. When the Dutch bought Manhattan Island from the Wappinger tribe, the price

    _____ only $24 worth of trinkets.

13. Now Manhattan _____ the center of a huge city.

14. New Amsterdam _____ the Dutch name for the area in the 1600s.

15. Today New York _____ the name for both the city and state.

Part 3

Circle the correct form of the verb *be* in ( ). Add information from the map on page 97 or the timeline below to complete each sentence correctly.

16. New York's five neighbor states (is/are) _____

    _____ .

17. The state's capital (is/are) _____ .

18. New York (was/were) one of the original thirteen states. It became a state in

    _____ .

New York History Timeline

Iroquois League formed.   Dutch settlers arrived.   English took over New Amsterdam and renamed it New York.   New York became our eleventh state.

| 1500s | 1624 | 1664 | 1788 |

Name _____

Looking Back

Read and Discover

The Mormons **wanted** religious freedom. They **travel** to Utah in 1847.

Circle the boldfaced verb that is correctly written in the past tense.

> The tense of a verb helps show when an action happens. **Past-tense verbs** show that an action happened in the past. Many past-tense verbs end in *-ed*. Irregular verbs change spelling in their past-tense form. Make sure the tense of each verb agrees with the time in which the action takes place. **Remember to use this information when you speak, too.**

See Handbook Section 17

Part 1

Underline the word or words in ( ) that fit in each sentence.

This monument to the sea gull, the Utah state bird, is in Salt Lake City.

1. Few people (live/lived) in the Utah desert in the 1840s.

2. In 1847 the Mormons (chose/will choose) the valley of the Great Salt Lake for their community.

3. The Mormons (suffered/suffer) hardships at first.

4. They worked hard to raise crops and (will make/made) the desert fertile through irrigation.

5. In the pioneers' second year in the valley, hungry grasshoppers (swarmed/swarm) over the fields and began eating the crops.

6. Sea gulls from the Great Salt Lake swooped down and (eat/ate) the grasshoppers.

7. The Mormons (built/build) a monument to the sea gulls in 1913.

8. In the 1850s, immigrants (sail/sailed) from Europe to join the Mormons.

9. Some (walked/walk) across the United States, pulling their belongings in handcarts.

10. These pioneers (struggle/struggled) over high mountains to reach Salt Lake City.

Looking Back

Part 2

Rewrite each sentence so that the verb in ( ) is in the correct tense.

11. Ellis Shipp (travel) to Utah in a covered wagon in 1852. _____

_____

12. In 1873 her baby daughter (die) because there was no doctor nearby. _____

_____

13. Ellis Shipp (attend) medical school in Philadelphia. _____

_____

14. She (become) a doctor at a time when few women practiced medicine. _____

_____

15. She (start) her own medical school in Salt Lake City. _____

_____

Part 3

Write the words you underlined in Part 1 in the blanks. Unscramble the letters in circles to complete this sentence.

Last summer in Utah, I ___ ___ ___ ___ ___ ___ ___ on the Great Salt Lake.

16. ___ ___ ___ ___ ___   21. ___ ◯ ___

17. ___ ◯ ___ ___   22. ___ ___ ◯ ___

18. ___ ___ ◯ ___   23. ___ ___ ___ ___ ◯

19. ___ ___ ___   24. ___ ◯ ___ ___

20. ___ ___ ___ ◯ ___   25. ___ ___ ___ ___ ___ ___

Name _____

Looking Back

Read and Discover

The weather in Vermont is not very warm. People there usually don't need no air conditioning.
Underline each word that means "no." Draw a star by the sentence that contains only one word that means "no."

A **negative** is a word that means "no" or "not." The words *no, not, nothing, none, never, nowhere,* and *nobody* are negatives. The negative word *not* is often found in contractions like *don't* or *wasn't*. Do not use two negatives in the same sentence. **Remember to use this information when you speak, too.**

See Handbook Section 22

Part 1

Circle each negative word below. Write *X* after each sentence that has too many negatives.

1. In the 1700s, settlers in Vermont couldn't agree about who should control the land. ____

2. Settlers who lived in Vermont couldn't never keep from fighting with newer settlers from New York. ____

3. The New Yorkers could not defeat the Vermont settlers, who called themselves the Green Mountain Boys. ____

Ethan Allen also fought against the British in the Revolutionary War.

4. The leader of the Green Mountain Boys, Ethan Allen, didn't never give up until the Vermont settlers controlled the land. ____

5. Vermont didn't become no state when the United States were formed in 1776. ____

6. Vermont settlers didn't want to be no part of the United States. ____

7. They created an independent republic that wasn't a part of no other nation. ____

8. Vermont did not join the Union until 1791. ____

9. Some people do not know that Vermont is one of the most beautiful states. ____

Part 2

Revise each sentence so it contains just one negative. There may be more than one correct way to do this.

10. Shanti didn't know nothing about the state of Vermont. _____

_____

11. Vermont's constitution was the first to say that nobody could own no enslaved

people. _____

_____

12. It is the only state in New England that does not have no coastline on the Atlantic

Ocean. _____

_____

13. None of the other states don't produce more of Shanti's favorite treat, maple syrup!

_____

_____

Part 3

Circle six negatives in the puzzle. Use one of them to write a sentence about your state.

N	O	T	H	I	N	G
R	N	K	V	U	E	N
N	O	T	Y	C	V	O
O	B	P	Z	B	E	K
N	O	W	H	E	R	E
E	D	H	R	B	O	U
N	Y	H	Q	Z	E	W

_____

_____

_____

_____

Name _____

Looking Back

Read and Discover

    a. West Virginia is **more big** than Rhode Island.
    b. North Dakota is **bigger** than West Virginia.
Which sentence uses the boldfaced word or phrase correctly? ____

> You can use an **adjective** to **compare** two people, places, or things. Just add -*er* to most adjectives with one syllable. Add the word *more* before most adjectives with two or more syllables. ◀📢 **Remember to use this information when you speak, too.**

See Handbook Sections 15 and 23

Part 1 ✏️

Underline the word or words in ( ) to complete each sentence.

1. West Virginia is (more mountainous/mountainouser) than most other states.

2. Do the mountains help make it (more beautiful/beautifuler) than anywhere else?

3. Until the Civil War, West Virginia was part of the (more large/larger) state of Virginia.

4. The people who lived in northwestern Virginia were (more unhappy/unhappier) with the state government than people in other parts of the state.

West Virginia joined the Union in 1863.

5. Virginia decided to join the Confederate States when the Civil War broke out, but people in the northwest were (more loyal/loyaler) to the Union.

6. They formed the (more small/smaller) state of West Virginia in 1863.

7. West Virginia has (richer/more rich) natural resources than some eastern states.

8. Coal deposits are (plentifuller/more plentiful) there than in surrounding states.

9. Mining was (more important/importanter) in West Virginia's past than it is today.

Part 2

Use a word from the word bank to complete each sentence correctly. You may need to change the form of the word or add the word *more*. (10–14)

important	dangerous	short	safe	risky

From the 1890s to the 1930s, many West Virginians worked in coal mines. Coal mining was _____ than most jobs. Many miners were killed in fires and accidents, and many got sick from breathing the coal dust. These jobs were _____ than they should have been. The workers were treated unfairly. Many miners were forced to work 10–14 hours a day for very little money. They formed unions to fight for _____ working days. They also demanded _____ working conditions.

Today, many West Virginians work in service industries. These include hotels, stores, and hospitals. Many tourists visit West Virginia each year, too. The tourist industry is _____ today than it was many years ago.

Part 3

West Virginia has many mountains, valleys, and rivers. It also has many natural resources, including coal, sand, gravel, salt, and natural gas. Write two sentences comparing West Virginia to your state. Use at least two comparative adjectives.

15. _____

_____

16. _____

_____

Name _____

Looking Back

Proofreading Others' Writing

Read this report about life in America's early days and find the mistakes. Use the proofreading marks below to show how each mistake should be fixed.

Proofreading Marks

Mark	Means	Example
⊙	add a period	New England has forests, lakes, and streams⊙
∧	add a comma	New England has forests∧lakes, and streams.
≡	make into a capital letter	New england has forests, lakes, and streams.
/	make into a lowercase letter	New England has forests, Lakes, and streams.
ℒ	take away	New England has forests, lakes, and and streams.
sp	fix spelling	New England has forests, lakes, and streems.

Colonial Life in New England

You know that the thirteen colonies became the first thirteen states. You might Not know what life was like in colonial times. Imagine living in a home where many of the things you use every day have to be made by hand. Many families didn't have no store-bought furniture or clothes. In a colonial home, clothing, candle, rugs, and furniture was usually homemade. So were toys sheets, and blankets. Children help with this work

In the colonies' early days, only boys and girls from wealthy families went to school? Some children were taught at home by private tutors. In 1647 the first public school was started in Massachusetts. In that year a law were passed. It said that any any town with fifty families or more had to build a school.

Jamestown, virginia was won of the first permanent settlements in New England. If you visit Jamestown today, you'll find a model of a colonial village. People dressed in colonial clothing showing visitors exactly what life was like in America's early days.

Proofreading Your Own Writing

You can use the list below to help you find and fix mistakes in your own writing. Write the titles of your own stories or reports in the blanks on top of the chart. Then use the questions to check your work. Make a check mark (✔) in each box after you have checked that item.

Titles

Proofreading Checklist for Unit 4

Have I used subject pronouns correctly? (*I, you, he, she, it, we, they*)				
Have I used object pronouns correctly? (*me, you, him, her, it, us, them*)				
Have I used *I* and *me* correctly when naming myself and another person?				
Do the subject and verb in every sentence agree?				
Have I avoided extra negatives?				

Also Remember . . .

Does each sentence begin with a capital letter?				
Does each sentence end with the right mark?				
Have I spelled each word correctly?				
Have I used commas correctly?				

Your Own List
Use this space to write your own list of things to check in your writing.

Name _____

Looking Back

Pronouns

Write the pronoun that could take the place of the underlined word or words in each sentence. If the pronoun would be the first word in a sentence, capitalize it.

1. <u>Mark and Alicia</u> wrote a report about New Mexico. _____

2. <u>Alicia</u> learned about a Native American group called the Basketmakers. _____

3. She read about <u>the Basketmakers</u> in a book about Chaco Canyon. _____

4. <u>Chaco Canyon</u> is a national historical park in New Mexico. _____

5. Alicia showed <u>Mark</u> some beautiful pictures of the ruins there. _____

6. She and <u>Mark</u> saw pictures of cliff dwellings. _____

7. The pictures amazed him and <u>Alicia</u>. _____

Circle the word or words in ( ) that will complete each sentence correctly.

8. (Me and my family/My family and I) want to visit Santa Fe, New Mexico.

9. The Chamber of Commerce sent (my brother and me/my brother and I) a brochure about Santa Fe.

10. (My brother and I/Me and my brother) want to visit the Palace of the Governors.

11. My uncle told (Randy and me/Randy and I) that it is one of the oldest buildings in the United States.

12. (This/This here) picture shows a Pueblo community.

13. (That/This) building over there was used in ceremonies.

Verbs and Comparative Adjectives

Choose a word in ( ) to correctly complete each sentence. Write the word on the line.

14. The frontiersman Kit Carson _____ in Taos, New Mexico. (live/lived)

15. Today Kit Carson's home _____ a museum. (is/are)

16. Tourists _____ Kit Carson's home and other historic sites in the Taos area. (visits/visit)

17. The Sangre de Cristo Mountains _____ to the north of the village of Taos. (is/are)

18. In 1821 New Mexico became part of Mexico, but in 1846 the United States _____ possession of the region. (takes/took)

19. When the Mexican War ended, a treaty _____ New Mexico to the United States. (gave/gives)

20. New Mexico _____ a state in 1912. (becomes/became)

21. Is New Mexico _____ than Texas? (larger/more large)

22. No, but New Mexico is _____ than Texas. (most mountainous/more mountainous)

Negatives

Cross out the extra negative in each sentence.

23. I haven't never visited a pueblo.

24. Don't take no photographs if you visit a Pueblo community.

25. Most Pueblo communities don't allow no photography or tape recordings.

Name _____

Looking Back

FAMILY LEARNING OPPORTUNITIES

In Unit 4 of *G.U.M.* we are learning how different kinds of words are used in sentences. The activities on these pages give extra practice with some of the concepts we're learning. You can help your child use the information he or she is learning in school by choosing one or more activities to complete with your child at home.

Let's Go! (Choosing Subject and Object Pronouns)

Ask your child to think about a place in your state he or she would like to visit with you and a friend. Then work with your child to write a few sentences about the trip using the pronouns *I* and *me*.

Example	Marianne and **I** would like to go to the Rock 'n' Roll Museum in Cleveland. My mom could drive Marianne and **me** there.

Word Search (Past-Tense Verbs)

Circle seven verbs in this puzzle.

```
F  Q  L  Z  R  V  J  N  X  S
O  W  I  C  Z  P  K  M  C  E
L  R  S  X  S  G  Q  V  R  R
L  T  T  V  T  I  S  T  V
O  Y  E  X  R  F  V  W  N  E
W  D  N  V  E  D  E  R  M  D
A  V  E  M  T  E  A  C  H  K
B  Z  D  Q  C  G  C  T  P  L
D  F  J  W  H  H  V  Y  D  X
F  G  K  R  E  A  C  H  E  D
Q  H  L  N  D  J  B  Z  V  M
```

Write the verbs that could tell about the past.

_____   _____

_____   _____

What ending do the four past-tense verbs have? _____

Looking Back

Name That Character (Subject Pronouns)

You can play this guessing game with the whole family. First choose a category, such as movies, TV shows, or books. Then take turns thinking of a character and giving clues about that character's identity. Each clue should begin with a subject pronoun. (Subject pronouns include *he, she, I, you, it, we,* and *they.*) Listeners can guess which character is being described.

Example	**He** has nerves of steel. **He** catches crooks. **They** usually get arrested.

Name That State (Forms of *Be*)

Work with your child to write riddles about some of the fifty states. Use a form of the verb *be* in each clue. (Forms of *be* include *is, are, was,* and *were.*) Scramble the name of the state you are thinking of and write the scrambled letters after the riddle.

Examples	This **is** the Aloha State. This state is ____ ____ ____ ____ ____ ____. (waiiaH)
	Flamingos **are** residents of this boot-shaped state.
	This state is ____ ____ ____ ____ ____ ____ ____. (lrdaioF)
	Gold **was** very important here in 1849.
	This state is ____ ____ ____ ____ ____ ____ ____ ____ ____ ____. (aioniarflC)

Caption Action (Past-Tense Verbs)

With your child, look at some photographs of a family vacation or trip you took together. Or, look at photographs of family celebrations. Help your child select three or four favorite pictures and write a caption for each one. Each caption should use a past-tense verb.

Examples	We **hiked** in the Rocky Mountains. I **saw** a moose in the moonlight. We **cooked** stew over a fire.

Name _____

Looking Back

Read and Discover

We just bought a new paint program.
Do you want to learn how to use it?
Press RETURN when you're ready to begin.
Wow, this program has so many gorgeous colors!
Which sentence gives a command? Circle its end mark.
Which sentence shows excitement? Circle its end mark.
Which sentence asks a question? Circle its end mark.
Which sentence makes a statement? Circle its end mark.

> Begin every sentence with a **capital letter**. Use a **period** to end a statement and a **question mark** to end a question. Use a **period** or an **exclamation point** to end a command. Use an **exclamation point** to end an exclamation.
>
> **See Handbook Section 9**

Part 1

Circle each capitalization or punctuation error.

1. the computer can store copies of paintings by several artists

2. May I change the colors and move the shapes.

3. do you want to fill in that circle with bright orange.

4. No, let's use brick red?

5. invent your own design

6. Wow, it's like painting on the screen.

7. Please show me your picture?

8. Press EXIT when you are finished

9. will the computer save my painting.

10. computer painting is the best invention ever!

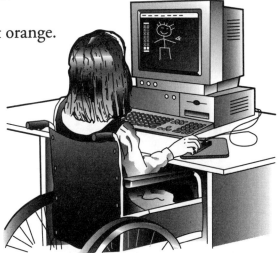

With a computer art program, you move the mouse to draw and add colors.

Grab Bag

Part 2

Complete this advertisement for a new computer art program. Write one statement, one question, one command, and one exclamation.

11. Have you ever wished _____

_____

12. Hi-Price Computing has just invented _____

_____

13. Try this _____

_____

14. What a fantastic _____

_____

Part 3

Add end punctuation to each clue. Then solve the riddle.

15. I am shaped like a square____

16. You look at me while you work on the computer____

17. I show you what you are doing on the computer____

18. Please keep me clean____

19. I am like a face for the computer____

20. What am I____

I am the ____ ____ ____ ____ ____ ____.

Grab Bag

Read and Discover

Steven Jobs founded Apple Computer Company in California with Stephen Wozniak. At the young age of 27, he was known as Chairman Steven Jobs.

Circle words that name specific people, places, or businesses. Underline a word that is used before someone's name to show respect for that person.

> A common noun names a person, place, or thing. A **proper noun** names a specific person, place, or thing. All the important words in proper nouns are capitalized. A **title of respect** is used before a person's name. Titles of respect include *Chairman* and *Mr.* They are also capitalized.

See Handbook Sections 1 and 14

Part 1

Draw a line through capital letters that should be small letters. Circle small letters that should be capital letters.

1. Steven jobs worked at a Video game company called atari.

2. He left the Company and traveled across india with a Friend named dan.

3. When jobs came back to california, he joined a computer Club.

4. There he met stephen wozniak.

5. Wozniak worked at hewlett-Packard corporation.

6. They started making little Computers in a garage and named their company apple.

7. In 1977 Apple moved to an Office on stevens Creek boulevard in cupertino.

8. Jobs left Apple in 1985.

9. The company had become one of the largest computer Manufacturers in the United States.

10. Today people across america use apple Products.

Grab Bag

Part 2

Underline the proper nouns in each sentence. Rewrite the sentence correctly.

11. I want to start a computer company with my friend amy berry. _____

_____

12. We have decided on the name berry pie computing. _____

_____

13. Someday we might have offices in chicago, illinois, or london, england. _____

_____

_____

14. Then amy will be president berry of berry pie computing. _____

_____

Part 3

Imagine you are the president of a computer company. Invent a name and an address for your company. Address this envelope to yourself.

Green Kangaroo Software Co.
1369 Timberjump Ln.
Los Angeles, CA 90077

_____

_____

_____

_____

Name _____

Grab  Bag

Read and Discover

Dr. Carl M. Peterson and Mr. Joseph R. Cleveland both teach computer classes at the local university.

Circle a short way to write *Doctor*. Draw a square around a short way to write *Mister*. Underline each letter that stands for a name.

> **Abbreviations** are short forms of words. Many titles of respect, such as *Doctor* or *Mister*, are abbreviated. An abbreviation usually begins with a capital letter and ends with a period. An **initial** is a capital letter with a period after it. An initial takes the place of a name. For example, the *F.* in *President John F. Kennedy* stands for President Kennedy's middle name, *Fitzgerald*.

See Handbook Sections 1 and 2

Part 1

Find the errors below. Circle each small letter that should be a capital letter. Draw a line through each capital letter that should be a small letter. Add periods where they are needed.

1. My neighbor, mr. Leo T Jackson, likes robots.

2. He lives around the corner

   from my house on Arden sT

3. Mr Jackson told me about a new robot.

4. He said that dr. John Bares helped design a

   robot that explores volcano craters.

Robots can explore areas where humans can't go yet.

5. His partner, Dr Whittaker, also helped design a robot to clean up nuclear waste.

6. The robot that dr Bares and DR. Whittaker designed is shaped like a spider.

7. My science teacher, mr. Peter s. Li, told my class about another robot.

8. Mr Li said that this robot helped train America's 1992 Olympic Table Tennis team.

9. My soccer coach, mrs. Ellen r Mayes, wishes we had a robot to help with practice.

Grab Bag

Part 2

Rewrite each name correctly. Abbreviate titles of respect.

10. mistress Margaret W. may _____

11. doctor leroy haggins _____

12. mister e c hui _____

13. ms zoila hidalgo _____

14. mistress Angela a. Capelli _____

15. doctor A. v. briggs _____

16. Mister everett castle _____

Part 3

Imagine you are a computer scientist. Write to Dr. Hacker at Hi-Price Computing Company to get information on her new invention, a robot waiter. Invent an address for your laboratory. Sign the letter with your title (*Dr., Mr.,* or *Ms.*), your first name, middle initial, and last name.

Dear _____ :

    Please send me information on your new robot waiter. The address of my laboratory is:

_____

_____

_____

_____

               Sincerely,

               _____

Name _____

Grab Bag

Read and Discover

In the movie Young Sherlock Holmes, computer animation created exciting effects. That movie was based on characters from Sir Arthur Conan Doyle's book a study in scarlet.
Underline the movie title. Circle the three letters in the book title that should be capitalized.

> Underline **book titles** and **movie titles**. Use quotation marks around the titles of **songs, poems,** and **stories.** Capitalize the first word, last word, and all the important words of any title. Always capitalize *is, are, was,* and *were* in titles. Do not capitalize *a, an, the, and, to, on, or, of,* or *with* unless that word is the first word or the last word in the title.

See Handbook Sections 1 and 3

Part 1

Underline each book title or movie title. Add quotation marks around the name of a song, story, or poem. Circle each small letter that should be a capital letter.

1. tron was the first movie to use computer effects.

2. The book jurassic park inspired a movie in which computer animation brought dinosaurs to life.

3. Older movies such as journey to the center of the Earth used models to represent dinosaurs.

4. That movie was based on a book by Jules Verne, who also wrote around the world in 80 days.

5. Computers erased pictures of Chevy Chase so that his clothes seemed to float in the movie memoirs of an invisible man.

Dinosaur experts helped computer animators make sure that dinosaurs in the movie <u>Jurassic Park</u> were realistic.

6. In the movie the lion king, animators made one wildebeest look like a stampede.

7. The song circle of life was written especially for this movie.

8. toy story was the first full-length film to be animated completely by computer.

Grab Bag

Part 2

Imagine that you work at a computer store that sells movies and books about computers. Invent a book or movie title to complete each sentence. Write it correctly.

9. Do you have the book _____ ?

10. Was that book written by the same person who wrote the book _____

    _____ ?

11. The best movie we have about computer games is _____

    _____ .

12. Here's a book about computer games called _____

    _____ .

13. This book is being made into a movie called _____

    _____ .

Part 3

Write a brief paragraph about a book or movie you liked. Write the title correctly.

_____

_____

_____

_____

_____

_____

Name _____

Grab Bag

Read and Discover

My aunt's computer is connected to the Internet. She's showing my cousins and me how to use it. We set up the computer in my cousins' room.

Circle the word in which an apostrophe (') stands for a missing letter. Underline two nouns in which an apostrophe shows ownership.

A **possessive noun** shows ownership. Add an **apostrophe** and *s* to a singular noun to show ownership (*Mrs. Wong's computer*). Add an apostrophe after the *s* of a plural noun (*my parents' computer*). Add an apostrophe and an *s* if the plural noun doesn't end in *s* (*women's computers*). A **contraction** is made of two words put together. An **apostrophe** takes the place of one or more letters. (*I am* becomes *I'm*.)

See Handbook Sections 7, 22, and 24

Part 1

Underline the correct word in each pair.

1. My (aunt's/aunts) computer is connected to the Internet.

2. The Internet connects (people's/peoples') computers all over the world.

3. (Its/It's) a system that lets people send computer messages.

4. (They're/Their) carried over wires and telephone lines.

5. The Internet lets (its/it's) users talk with others who share their special interests.

6. These (groups'/group's) interests range from sports to archaeology to space travel.

7. People (don't/dont') have trouble finding others to communicate with on the Internet.

8. Maybe (your/you're) one of the 20 million people who are connected to the Internet today.

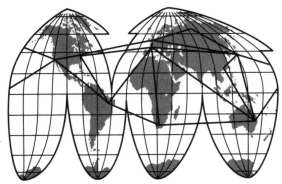

The Internet is an international network of computers.

Part 2

Rewrite each set of boldfaced words as a contraction or a phrase that includes a possessive noun.

9. Have you received **the message from my brother** yet? _____

_____

10. **He is** visiting his friends. _____

11. **The computer belonging to his friends** is hooked up to the Internet. _____

_____

12. **I am** sending my brother a message. _____

13. He **does not** know that I know how to use E-mail. _____

_____

14. **He will** be very surprised. _____

15. **Is not** the Internet great? _____

16. **The computer belonging to my sister** is very powerful. _____

_____

17. The E-mail **address of my sister** has her initials in it. _____

_____

Part 3

Write a message you would like to send a friend on the Internet. Use at least one possessive noun and one contraction in your message.

_____

Name _____

Grab Bag

Read and Discover

Some computer programs bring together writing, photos, sound, and video.

Find four items in a series in this sentence. What punctuation mark follows each of the first three items? _____

Artists writers and computer programmers work together to create multimedia programs.

Find three items in a series in this sentence. What punctuation mark should follow each of the first two items? _____

A **series** is a list of three or more words or phrases. Commas are used to separate the items in a series. The last comma in a series goes before the word *and* or the word *or*.

See Handbook Section 8

Part 1

Add commas where they are needed below. Cross out commas that should not be there.

1. There are multimedia programs about nature history music and other topics.

2. A multimedia program lets you decide what to do, when to do it and how to do it.

3. You could read a play watch a video of actors, or see pictures of a theater.

4. Jordan David Elaine and, I tried a multimedia program called "Math on Mars."

5. The game teaches players to add subtract, multiply and, divide.

6. Math problems, videos of a math expert and cartoons of Martians, appear on the screen.

7. The math expert explains addition if you push a button, type "add," and, click OK.

8. Players decide whether to count the Martians' ears eyes hands or feet.

Addition Quiz: 5 + 6 = _?_

Multimedia programs use words, animation, photographs, and video to provide information.

Grab Bag

Part 2 ✏️

Combine four sentences into one. Each new sentence should have three commas in it.

The Martians have red feet.   The Martians have golden eyes.
The Martians have blue teeth.   The Martians have lavender toenails.

9. _____

_____

_____

To start the game turn on the computer.   To start the game open the program.
To start the game enter your name.   To start the game press RETURN.

10. _____

_____

_____

Part 3 ✏️

Your job is to design a new Martian for "Math on Mars." Draw your Martian below.
Then write a sentence telling what it looks like. Use three words from the word bank.

| lumpy | puffy | pointy | squishy | hairy | glassy | curly | scaly |

_____

_____

_____

_____

_____

_____

Name _____

Grab Bag

Read  and Discover

Yes, we have a new word processing program. Tim, show the class how to choose the program. No, I don't think that is the correct icon. Well, you were right after all.

Circle the commas. Write the word that comes before each comma.

_____   _____   _____   _____

Use a **comma** to show a pause in a sentence. When a sentence begins with an **introductory word**, such as *Yes, No,* or *Well,* put a comma after that word. If a sentence starts with someone's name and the sentence is spoken to that person, write a comma after that person's name.

See Handbook Section 8

Part 1

Add a comma where it belongs in each sentence below.

1. "James please show the class how to move words on the computer," said Mrs. Huey.

2. "Yes I think that is the right way to erase a whole line of words," she added.

3. "No a word processing program does not have an imagination," she said.

4. "Toshia press DELETE now," Mrs. Huey said.

5. "Robin do you know how to save your work?" Max asked.

6. "No the computer cannot tell the difference

   between good and bad writing," Mrs. Huey explained.

7. "Well maybe I do need to learn to write well," Robin said.

8. "Yes that's a good idea!" Max responded.

9. "Josh have you turned the program off?" Toshia asked.

10. "Yes I clicked on QUIT to exit," Josh answered.

Writers have composed with quill pens and typewriters. Many modern writers use word processors.

Grab Bag

123

G.U.M.

Part 2

Imagine you're having a conversation with a boy named Tim. Write *Yes, No, Well,* or *Tim* to begin each sentence below. Make sure to use a comma correctly in each sentence.

11. "_____ do you know how to use the spell check?" I asked.

12. "_____ I learned how to use it yesterday," he answered.

13. "_____ is it hard to use this feature?" I wanted to know.

14. "_____ it's very easy," he answered.

15. "_____ I guess all of us should learn how," I decided.

Part 3

Write two questions and two answers about computers on the lines below. Begin each sentence with *Yes, No, Well,* or a person's name.

Question: _____

_____

Answer: _____

_____

_____

Question: _____

_____

Answer: _____

_____

_____

Name _____

124

G.U.M.

Grab Bag

Read and Discover

In February of 1996 an unusual chess match was played. One player was human, and the other player was a computer. Underline the sentence that contains two complete thoughts. Circle the word that joins the two thoughts.

> A **compound sentence** is made of two simple sentences joined by a conjunction such as *and*, *or*, or *but*. Use a **comma** before the conjunction.

See Handbook Sections 8, 12, and 21

Part 1

Underline each compound sentence. Add a comma before the conjunction in each compound sentence. (1–8)

Scientists at IBM created a special computer chip just for chess. They put this chip inside a powerful computer and they named the computer Deep Blue. Because they wanted to test Deep Blue, they called chess master Garry Kasparov. The scientists challenged Kasparov to a chess match and he agreed.

Garry Kasparov is the world chess champion. He had played chess against computers before and twice the computers had won. Kasparov still believed he could beat Deep Blue.

Deep Blue and Kasparov played six games in the match. Each player had to complete the first 40 moves in two hours and Kasparov had to race against time. Deep Blue can calculate about 200 million moves a second but a human player can't think that quickly.

Deep Blue won the first game but Kasparov won the second. The third and fourth games were tied. Kasparov beat Deep Blue in the fifth game. Chess fans around the world watched. Would Kasparov win or would Deep Blue be the champion? Kasparov won the final game and human beings everywhere cheered.

Grab Bag

Part 2

Rewrite each pair of sentences as one compound sentence. Use *and, or,* or *but* correctly in each sentence. Remember to use a comma before the conjunction.

9. Kasparov beat Deep Blue. It took him six games. _____

    _____

10. Some say this was a contest of humans against machines. Others see it differently.

    _____

    _____

11. Humans built the computer. Human thinking makes it work. _____

    _____

    _____

Part 3

Use the clues to help you complete the crossword puzzle.

Across

3. *And, but,* and *or* are __.
4. A comma goes __ a conjunction.
5. A __ separates items in a series.

Down

1. Join two simple __ with *and, but,* or *or* to make a compound sentence.
2. We wanted to stay longer at the show, __ we had to go home.
3. A __ sentence is made of two simple sentences.

Name _____

Grab Bag

Read and Discover

The artist said, "I create animated cartoons on my computer."
The artist said that she creates cartoons on her computer.
Which sentence shows a speaker's exact words? Circle it.
Circle the marks that come before and after the speaker's
exact words.

A **direct quotation** is a speaker's exact words. Use quotation marks around a speaker's words in a direct quotation. An **indirect quotation** retells a speaker's words. The word *that* usually comes before the speaker's words in an indirect quotation. Do not use quotation marks in an indirect quotation.

See Handbook | Section 4

Part 1

Add quotation marks to the sentences that contain direct quotations. Write *I* next to sentences that contain indirect quotations.

1. I said that I want to draw a duck flying. ____

2. The artist said, Let's draw the duck's wings in several different positions. ____

3. If the computer shows a series of pictures, the wings seem to flap, she explained. ____

4. The artist said that changes in background make the duck seem to fly forward. ____

5. I'll draw clouds in the air and a barn on the ground, I said. ____

6. Don't forget to make the barn small, because it's far away, she said. ____

7. She added that nearby objects should be drawn larger than far away objects. ____

8. She said, This is called *perspective*. ____

9. I told her that I liked the finished drawing. ____

10. It looks so real! I said. ____

Computers can make a drawing seem to move.

Grab Bag

Part 2

Rewrite each indirect quotation as a direct quotation. Put quotation marks around the speaker's exact words. Don't forget to begin each quotation with a capital letter.

11. The artist told me that the computer stores many voices and sounds. _____

_____

_____

12. I said that I'd like to record a real duck quacking. _____

_____

13. She said that her friend at the zoo might let us visit the ducks on Saturday. _____

_____

_____

14. I said that I'd like to bring my tape recorder along. _____

_____

Part 3

Follow the dots to find the picture. Then write something a computer artist might say about the picture. Use a direct quotation.

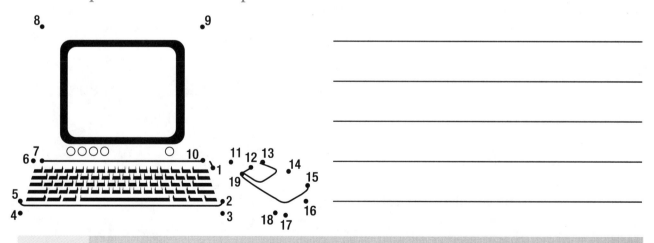

Name _____

Grab Bag

Read  and Discover

a. "We're going to Mr. Lee's computer store to try a virtual reality game," said Rob.
b. Jamie added "I've heard you can fly like a bird in virtual reality"

Which sentence is written correctly? Circle the two places in the second sentence where punctuation marks belong.

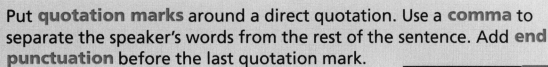

Put **quotation marks** around a direct quotation. Use a **comma** to separate the speaker's words from the rest of the sentence. Add **end punctuation** before the last quotation mark.

See Handbook Section 4

Part 1

Put a *C* next to each sentence that uses quotation marks, commas, and end marks correctly. Add the missing punctuation marks to the other sentences.

1. "Virtual reality is an imaginary world created by computer" Mr. Lee told us. ___

2. "How does it work" asked Jamie. ___

3. Mr. Lee said "Put on this helmet and these gloves" ___

4. "The helmet places computer screens in front of Jamie's eyes" he explained ___

5. I asked, "What are the gloves for" ___

6. "They tell the computer how Jamie is moving her hands," said Mr. Lee. ___

7. "Wow, I'm petting a unicorn in a forest!" Jamie shouted. ___

8. Rob asked "What is virtual reality used for" ___

9. "People can learn to fly a plane without leaving the ground," said Mr. Lee. ___

A virtual reality helmet allows people to enter a world where almost anything is possible.

Grab Bag

Part 2 ✏️

Finish these sentences. Write three other things Jamie might say about her experience and one question you could ask. Use commas, quotation marks, and end marks correctly.

10. Jamie said _____

_____

11. I asked _____

_____

12. _____

_____ Jamie answered.

13. She added _____

_____

Part 3 ✏️

Rewrite the sentences below. Add missing punctuation marks. Begin a new paragraph with each change of speaker.

We're headed straight for a meteor Jana shouted. Turn the spaceship to the left Mick ordered. That seemed close Jana said as she took her helmet off. It seemed close, but it wasn't real Mick said.

_____

_____

_____

_____

_____

_____

Name _____

Grab Bag

Proofreading Others' Writing

Read this report about the history of computers and find the mistakes. Use the proofreading marks below to show how each mistake should be fixed.

Proofreading Marks

Mark	Means	Example
∧	add	I ^like^ our new computer.
≡	make into a capital letter	i̲ like our new computer.
/	make into a lowercase letter	I like Øur new computer.
⊙	add a period	I like our new computer⊙
⋏	add a comma	Yes⋏ I like our new computer.
⋁	add quotation marks	⋁I like our new computer,⋁ she said.
(sp)	fix spelling	I (sp)loke our new computer.

The History of the Computer

Last weekend Alices father took us to the science museum. We saw a computer exhibit There were displays of computer art, talking computers, and screens you could touch.

Our guide was doctor Ted s Novak. Dr. Novak told us about the history of computers. He said that the first invention that helped people solve math problems was the abacus. the Babylonians used beads on a frame to help count cattle and other goods 5,000 years ago.

the abacus cant follow instructions like a computer," Dr. Novak explained. "But it's still useful for adding, subtracting, multiplying, And dividing"

Dr Novak said that the first electronic computer was built in Great britain to break enemy codes during World War II. Early computers were as big as entire rooms and they weighed as much as 30 tons. The invention of the microchip made computers smaller cheaper, and more efficient. Personal computers appeared in 1975, and now there are about 100 million compures in the world. After the tour we watched a movie called how computers work. Then, just before it was time to go, we had a chance to take a virtual reality hike on the surface of venus. Yes that was exciting!

Proofreading Your Own Writing

You can use the list below to help you find and fix mistakes in your own writing. Write the titles of your own stories or reports in the blanks on top of the chart. Then use the questions to check your work. Make a check mark (✓) in each box after you have checked that item.

Titles

Proofreading Checklist for Unit 5

Have I capitalized proper nouns and all the important words in titles?				
Have I placed quotation marks around each speaker's exact words?				
Have I used commas correctly to separate items in a series and after introductory words?				
Have I joined each compound sentence with a comma followed by a conjunction?				

Also Remember . . .

Does each sentence begin with a capital letter and end with the right mark?				
Do all abbreviations begin with a capital letter and end with a period?				
Have I used possessives correctly?				
Have I used contractions correctly?				

Your Own List

Use this space to write your own list of things to check in your writing.

Name _____

Grab Your Bag

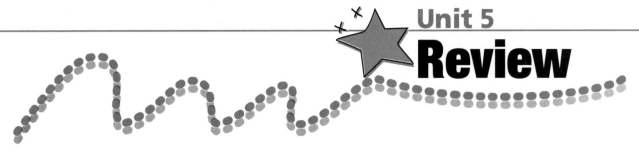

Punctuation and Capitalization

Draw three lines (≡) under each small letter that should be capitalized. Draw a line through each capital letter that should be a small letter. Cross out punctuation that is wrong. Add commas, quotation marks, and end punctuation so each sentence is correct.

1. do you have a paint program on your computer!

2. no, but I wish I did

3. Try drawing a picture with my paint program?

4. The arcticwear clothing Company does all their business from a small factory in Anchorage, alaska.

5. The head of the company, president Marcia robards, designs the Clothes on her computer.

6. Mr Bradley f Waters owns a clothing store on Lawnwood ave.

7. He sold a parka made by Arcticwear clothing Company to dr Jean h Ashby.

8. Donald's computer can make the sound of a dog barking a frog croaking, or, a bird chirping.

9. His mother his brother and his sister keep asking Donald if there are animals living in his room.

10. Each time they ask, he says "No I don't have any pets in here."

11. Yesterday his mother, said "Donald what are those noises?"

12. Donald clicked his mouse and, his computer made a noise like an elephant.

13. Donald's mother was surprised for a moment but then she smiled.

Grab Bag

More Punctuation

Write *C* next to each sentence that is correctly punctuated. Add quotation marks if they are needed.

14. Your essay is very interesting, said the computer. ____

15. I can't believe my computer just spoke to me! Angela yelled. ____

16. Angela's sister told her that she must have imagined it. ____

Add missing punctuation marks to each sentence.

17. Lisa asked Is this a computer or a printer?

18. This is a computer with a printer attached to it explained Shawn.

Titles

Underline each book or movie title. Put quotation marks around each song, poem, or story title. Circle each capitalization error.

19. Before I read the book computer jazz, I had no idea that people could compose music on their computers.

20. The music for my favorite movie, the adventures Of Cyberella, was composed on computer.

21. The movie's theme song is called under the martian sky.

Possessives and Contractions

Underline the correct word in each pair.

22. This (computer's/computers') memory is too small for this CD-ROM game.

23. (Lets'/Let's) add more memory to the hard drive.

24. (Isnt/Isn't) that hard to do?

25. No, I added memory to my (parents'/parents) computer.

Name _____

Grab Bag

FAMILY LEARNING OPPORTUNITIES

In Unit 5 of *G.U.M.* we are learning which letters to capitalize and how to use punctuation marks such as periods, commas, and quotation marks. The activities on this page give extra practice with some of the concepts we're learning. You can help your child use the information he or she is learning in school by choosing one or more activities to complete with your child at home.

Lights, Camera, Action! (Proper Nouns and Titles of Respect)

Have your child create a movie poster for his or her favorite movie. The poster should include the movie's title, the names of the main characters, and the names of some of the actors and actresses who are in the movie. Have your child demonstrate the right way to write a movie title and then explain why certain words should be capitalized.

Newscast (Apostrophes)

Ask your child to imagine that he or she is a radio newscaster, and then write a brief news bulletin describing a recent event involving other members of the family. Ask him or her to include at least one contraction and one possessive noun in the bulletin. (Contractions include *don't* and *she's*. Possessive nouns include *grandparents'* and *family's*.) Encourage your child to broadcast the report for the family.

> ### News Broadcast
>
> Randy's class put on a play called <u>Peter and the Wolf</u>. Randy played the part of the wolf. Mom, Grandma, and I went to see the play. We thought it was great. Mom brought her camera, and I can't wait to see how the pictures turned out.

Interview **(Commas After Introductory Words)**

Write four or five yes-or-no questions about a topic that is of interest to your child. Ask your child to write one-sentence answers to the questions. Encourage him or her to include at least four sentences that use commas after the introductory words *Yes, Well,* or *No.*

Comic Conversation **(Writing Direct Quotations)**

Ask your child to choose a comic strip from a local newspaper. Have your child cut out the comic strip and glue it on an 8^1/$_2$" x 11" sheet of paper so there is room to write below the comic strip. Then have your child rewrite the words the characters say as direct quotations. Remind your child to use quotation marks and commas correctly. Also remind him or her to begin a new paragraph with every change of speaker.

Imaginary Encounter **(Direct and Indirect Quotations)**

Invite your child to think of a famous person from any time in history. Ask your child to imagine what he or she would say to that person if they could meet. Then have your child write a brief dialogue recording this imaginary conversation. Encourage your child to use quotation marks and correct punctuation. Remind him or her to begin a new paragraph with every change of speaker.

Why This Comma? **(Commas in a Series; Commas After Introductory Words; Commas in Compound Sentences)**

Help your child cut out a short article from a newspaper or magazine. Then invite your child to point out various capital letters and punctuation marks in the piece of writing and explain why they are there.

| Examples | This comma joins two compound sentences.
This word is capitalized because it is a proper noun. |

Name _____

Grab Bag

Lesson 1 Add the correct end mark to each sentence.

1. Come to our garage sale on Saturday__

2. What are you going to sell__

3. We'll sell old toys, clothes, and furniture__

4. What a strange chair__

5. It's shaped like an elephant__

6. Do you think anyone will buy that elephant chair__

7. Come sit on it__

8. That jigsaw puzzle costs only five cents__

9. Are any of the puzzle pieces missing__

10. Wow, somebody just paid five dollars for that weird chair__

Lesson 2 Circle the complete subject and underline the complete predicate in each sentence.

1. People have studied dolphins for years.

2. The ancient Greeks drew pictures of dolphins.

3. Dolphins are very intelligent.

4. Dolphins travel in groups.

5. They talk to each other with whistles and clicks.

6. Dolphins have a very good sense of hearing.

7. Young dolphins stay with their mothers for over a year.

8. Dolphins help injured dolphins sometimes.

9. They support the injured dolphin with their fins.

10. Dolphins are related to whales.

Extra Practice

Lesson 3 Underline the complete subject in each sentence. Circle the simple subject.

1. Caitlyn's class made plaster sand fossils.

2. The students went to the beach.

3. The wet sand was perfect for molding.

4. The eager students drew fish skeletons in the sand.

5. Caitlyn's teacher mixed the wet plaster.

6. Caitlyn poured plaster over each sand drawing.

7. The sticky plaster dried overnight.

8. The excited students dug up their fossils in the morning.

9. The loose sand fell off.

10. The plaster fossils looked great on the classroom wall.

Lesson 4 In each sentence, underline the complete predicate. Circle the simple predicate.

1. My brother Marco has a new after-school job.

2. He works at Mr. Kim's grocery store.

3. Almost everyone shops at Mr. Kim's.

4. He sells the best produce in town.

5. My brother stacks fruits and vegetables.

6. He carries some very heavy boxes.

7. My brother is on the swim team.

8. The team visits Puerto Rico each spring.

9. Many team members have after-school jobs.

10. They earn money for the trip that way.

Name _____

Lesson 5 Circle the direct object in each sentence. The direct object receives the action of the underlined verb.

1. The batter <u>hit</u> the ball.

2. The shortstop <u>threw</u> the ball.

3. The first baseman <u>tagged</u> the base with his foot.

4. The ball <u>hit</u> the batter's leg.

5. The batter <u>rubbed</u> his sore leg.

6. The nervous pitcher <u>chewed</u> his gum.

7. Then the pitcher <u>threw</u> a perfect pitch.

8. The pitch <u>surprised</u> the batter.

9. The batter <u>swung</u> the bat.

10. He <u>missed</u> the ball completely.

Lesson 6 Underline the prepositional phrase that tells more about each boldfaced verb. Circle the preposition that begins each phrase.

1. We **flew** to San Francisco.

2. Our plane **swooped** over the San Francisco Bay.

3. We **sailed** on a ferryboat.

4. The ferryboat **went** across the bay.

5. Sea lions **swam** in the water.

6. We **walked** through Chinatown.

7. We **stepped** into a hotel's glass elevator.

8. The elevator **went** to the top floor.

9. We **ate** in a revolving restaurant.

10. We **looked** at the twinkling city lights.

Lesson 7 Write *I* after each incomplete sentence and *C* after each complete sentence. Then reread each incomplete sentence. Write *S* if the subject is missing and *P* if the predicate is missing.

1. My mother, my brothers, and I. ____ ____

2. Our family goes camping in the summertime. ____ ____

3. A very pretty campsite. ____ ____

4. Go camping every year. ____ ____

5. Mom finds a flat spot for our tent. ____ ____

6. The bright, warm campfire. ____ ____

7. Roast marshmallows and tell stories. ____ ____

8. Our sleeping bags keep us warm. ____ ____

9. Should never leave food out overnight. ____ ____

10. Hungry bears might find it. ____ ____

Lesson 8 Read each pair of sentences. Write a check mark after the sentence that gives more information.

1. a. Long ago people lived on cliffs. ____

   b. The ancestors of the Pueblo Indians built their homes on the sides of cliffs. ____

2. a. Recent discoveries have given us new information about the cliff dwellers' lives. ____

   b. Archaeologists have found cotton garments, leather sandals, bows and arrows, and mummies from the cliff dwellers' culture. ____

3. a. Cliff villages centered around *kivas,* brightly painted underground chambers. ____

   b. A lot of cliff villages had special rooms. ____

4. a. Cliff dwellers built rooms in different shapes. ____

   b. The eastern cliff dwellers built round *kivas,* and the western and southern cliff dwellers built rectangular ones. ____

5. a. There were many ways to climb up to the cliff dwellings. ____

   b. Ladders, steps, and winding paths led to the dwellings. ____

Lesson 9 Write *C* next to each compound sentence. Circle the conjunction in each compound sentence.

1. Each year our town holds a fishing contest, and this year I entered it. ___

2. I like fishing a lot. ___

3. I fished for hours, but I didn't catch anything. ___

4. The sun shone brightly, and the tops of my arms got sunburned. ___

5. I wore a wide-brimmed hat. ___

6. My face wasn't sunburned. ___

7. I knew I had to catch something, or I would lose the contest. ___

8. Something tugged on my line, but it was just an old tire. ___

9. I felt discouraged, but I kept on trying. ___

10. Finally, I caught a beautiful striped bass. ___

Lesson 10 Write a check mark after each sentence that is written correctly. Write *RO* after each run-on sentence and *CS* after each comma splice.

1. We had a family reunion at a ranch it was called the White Sun Ranch. ___

2. I rode a horse called Lightning, but he didn't move very quickly. ___

3. My grandmother and I woke up early we both watched the sun rise. ___

4. We took a family photo, all the kids lined up by size. ___

5. My cousin climbed a date tree, and he handed the dates down to us. ___

6. We ate cereal with chocolate milk in the ranch dining hall. ___

7. There were orange groves, we played hide and seek between the rows. ___

8. The two waitresses in the dining hall were twins they wore cowgirl outfits. ___

9. It was wintertime, but it was warm in the afternoons. ___

10. We stayed for a week I became good friends with my cousins. ___

Name _____

Lesson 11 Circle the boldfaced words that are nouns.

1. A **swamp** is a wet and **muddy** area.

2. Most swamps are **surrounded** by trees and **shrubs**.

3. Many forms of **plants** and animals live **in** swamps.

4. A swamp **may** be home to **turtles**, snakes, fish, and frogs.

5. Some swamps contain many **dangerous** animals, birds, and **reptiles**.

6. Alligators, snapping turtles, and water moccasins are dangerous **creatures** that **thrive** in these areas.

7. Water lilies and other thick **shrubs** grow well in the **moist** swamp floor.

8. Some swamps that contain salt **water** are **called** mangrove swamps.

9. They are **named** after the mangrove **trees** that grow there.

10. **Pelicans**, snails, and **other** sea animals live in mangrove swamps.

Lesson 12 Circle the proper nouns in these sentences.

1. Last August, my mother and I visited the city of Santa Fe in New Mexico.

2. We took a bus to get there.

3. Many *fiestas*, or festivals, are held in August.

4. At the Fiesta de Santa Fe, we watched Native Americans perform a ceremonial dance.

5. We saw traditional art at the Wheelwright Museum.

6. One of the oldest roads in the United States begins in Santa Fe.

7. The road is called El Camino Real.

8. It runs from Santa Fe to Chihuahua, a large city in Mexico.

9. The oldest government building in the United States is also in Santa Fe.

10. It is called the Palace of the Governors.

Lesson 13 Circle the boldfaced plural nouns and underline the boldfaced singular nouns in these sentences.

1. Joaquin has a very busy **schedule**.

2. He has piano **lessons** on Monday and Wednesday **afternoons**.

3. He gets up early in the **morning** and delivers **newspapers** in his **neighborhood**.

4. After **school** on Thursdays he tutors three **students** in math.

5. On Tuesdays Joaquin visits his **grandparents** and eats **dinner** with them.

6. On Friday **nights** Joaquin goes out for dinner with his **parents** and his sisters.

7. His **sisters** usually choose the **restaurant**.

8. Then the **family** watches **movies** at home.

9. On Saturday **mornings**, Joaquin's **sisters** sleep in until ten.

10. Then they help their **father** make **breakfast**.

Lesson 14 Circle each personal pronoun. Underline each possessive pronoun.

1. Cicadas have colored markings on their bodies.

2. They make a buzzing sound.

3. Each species of cicada has its own song.

4. Cicadas make their sound by moving a thin layer of skin.

5. A female cicada lays her eggs on the twigs of trees and shrubs.

6. When they hatch, the young fall to the ground.

7. When cicadas are young, they are called *nymphs*.

8. Each nymph climbs a tree and sheds its skin.

9. My family heard cicadas on a hike near the lake.

10. We all listened to their beautiful song.

Name _____

Extra Practice

Lesson 15 Underline the interrogative pronoun that belongs in each sentence.

1. (Who/What) wants to make chocolate chip cookies?

2. (Which/What) goes into the cookie batter?

3. (Which/What) is the yolk, the yellow part or the white part?

4. (Who/What) ate all the chocolate chips?

5. (What/Which) of these spoons is best for stirring the batter?

6. (Which/Who) wants to go outside while the cookies are baking?

7. (What/Which) will happen if we forget the cookies are in the oven?

8. (Which/What) is that unpleasant smell?

9. (What/Who) likes to eat burnt cookies?

10. (Which/What) cookie is burnt less, this one or that one?

Lesson 16 Underline each boldfaced linking verb. Circle each boldfaced action verb.

1. My dad and I **went** to the lake.

2. By noon, we **were** very hungry.

3. We **packed** tuna sandwiches for lunch.

4. My dad **is** a great cook.

5. His tuna sandwiches **are** the best in the world!

6. The recipe **is** very simple.

7. First you **toast** four pieces of bread.

8. Next you **stir** tuna, mayonnaise, and a pinch of pepper together in a bowl.

9. Then you **spread** the tuna mixture on the toast.

10. The sandwiches **are** ready.

Name _____

Lesson 17 Underline the main verb and circle the helping verb in each sentence.

1. This has been a great softball season for the Mighty Eagles.

2. They have won every game this year.

3. Last season the Eagles were having a tough time.

4. This year they may win the Silver Softball award.

5. Anna Gonzalez has set a record for the most runs.

6. Eric and Rita are catching very well in the outfield.

7. Ariel has been sick for a week.

8. In the next game, Hannah will pitch in her place.

9. Coach Snider will lead the school in a team spirit parade.

10. The whole school will cheer loudly for the Eagles.

Lesson 18 Circle the adjectives and underline the adverbs in the paragraph below. Write them on the lines.

The loon flew silently over the lake. It landed gently on the smooth water. The loon let out a lonesome cry. Across the lake a loon softly answered the cry. The sun set quickly. The sky sparkled with bright stars. The calm surface of the lake looked like a mirror. The moonlight made a shiny trail on the water. The loons quietly called to each other.

Adjectives	Adverbs
1. _____	6. _____
2. _____	7. _____
3. _____	8. _____
4. _____	9. _____
5. _____	10. _____

Lesson 19 Underline the prepositional phrase in each sentence. Circle each preposition.

1. Tammy and Caroline changed into their bathing suits.

2. They dragged the hose out of the garage.

3. They twisted the sprinkler onto the hose.

4. Caroline leaped through the sprinkler's fountain.

5. Tammy jumped over the dog.

6. She and Caroline ran around the sprinkler.

7. They threw a ball over the water.

8. The dog jumped at the ball.

9. The dog caught the ball in its mouth.

10. Later, everyone rested under a tree.

Lesson 20 Circle the conjunctions in the following sentences.

1. For my birthday, my aunt gave me a fish tank, and my grandpa gave me a gift certificate for some fish.

2. My sister wants the tank in her room, but I think it should go in the den.

3. My mom said I could buy three large fish or several smaller ones.

4. I also need fish food and pebbles for the bottom of the tank.

5. My gift certificate won't pay for everything, but I saved some allowance money to cover the rest.

6. The fish tank can be filled with fresh water or salt water.

7. Most fish can only live in one or the other.

8. My dad and I are going to the pet store tomorrow.

9. We wanted to go today, but it was closed.

10. I can't wait to pick out my new fish and put them in the tank!

Name _____

Lesson 21 Fill in each blank with *your* or *you're*. Remember to capitalize the first word in a sentence.

1. "Louis, _____ mother and I are going shopping," said Mr. Hall.

2. "Please take care of _____ little sister while we're out," he added.

3. "May I take Janey to the park while _____ gone?" Louis asked.

4. "Only if you and your sister wear _____ coats," answered Mrs. Hall.

5. Louis said, "Janey, _____ going to the park with me."

6. "May I ride on _____ shoulders?" Janey asked.

7. "_____ too heavy to carry," Louis said.

8. When Janey started to cry, Louis said, "Janey, _____ a big girl now."

9. "We can't go to the park if _____ going to cry," he added.

10. "I'll hold _____ hand while we walk there," Louis said kindly.

Lesson 22 Circle the word in ( ) that belongs in each sentence.

1. "I saw a flash of lightning over (their/they're/there)," said Emil.

2. "I hope Neil and Mel get back from (their/they're/there) hike soon," Sasha said.

3. "(Their/They're/There) experienced hikers," Emil responded.

4. "I hope this weather won't ruin (their/they're/there) science project," said Sasha.

5. "(Their/They're/There) two of the best science students in our class."

6. "(Their/They're/There) plan was to collect seeds in the forest today," Sasha continued.

7. "If they have to come home early, they may not be able to complete (their/they're/there) display of seed pods."

8. "I see Neil over (there/their/they're)!" Emil cried.

9. "(Their/They're/There) back!" shouted Sasha with relief.

10. Mel held up two small bags and said, "(Their/They're/There) both full of seeds!"

Name _____

Lesson 23 Write *its* or *it's* to complete each sentence correctly. Remember to begin a sentence with a capital letter.

1. "_____ so clear tonight. I bet we could see 1,000 stars," said Lois.

2. "Under good conditions, _____ actually possible to see as many as 2,000 stars in the night sky," said Charley.

3. "Look, there's a constellation!" Lois said. "Do you know _____ name?"

4. "That's Orion, the hunter. _____ named after a character in a Greek myth," answered Charley.

5. "Three bright stars mark _____ belt," he explained.

6. Charley went on, "Orion is at _____ highest point in the sky right now."

7. "We can see Orion when _____ wintertime," he explained.

8. "_____ not possible to see all the constellations at once," Charley said.

9. "As Earth rotates on _____ axis, different constellations come into view."

10. "_____ easy to see why people are fascinated with the stars," said Lois.

Lesson 24 Underline a word in ( ) to complete each sentence correctly.

1. The weather report (is/are) on TV right now.

2. I think weather reports (is/are) fascinating.

3. That announcer (is/are) my favorite.

4. A cold front (is/are) coming toward us.

5. The cold air (is/are) from Canada.

6. Yesterday the weather (was/were) mild.

7. Many people (was/were) picnicking by the lake.

8. The lake (was/were) frozen last year.

9. Now the lake (is/was) free of ice.

10. I think spring (is/are) on the way.

Lesson 25 Write *good* or *well* on the line to complete each sentence correctly.

1. I saw a _____ movie about an Arctic explorer last night.

2. The main actor played his part _____.

3. I think he's a _____ actor.

4. He was a _____ athlete in college.

5. He played basketball _____.

6. He was _____ at other things besides sports.

7. He did _____ in all his classes.

8. He had a _____ speaking voice, and so his English teacher suggested

   that he try out for a school play.

9. He performed so _____ that the audience gave him a standing ovation.

10. He is a _____ role model as well as a great actor.

Lesson 26 Write *doesn't* or *don't* on the lines to complete each sentence correctly.
Remember to capitalize the first word in a sentence.

1. "Since I _____ have a camera, may I borrow yours?" Raul asked Ramón.

2. "_____ Dusty have a camera?" Ramón asked.

3. "Dusty's camera was stolen, and he _____ have enough money to buy a

   new one," Raul said.

4. "Okay, you may borrow it, but _____ lose it," Ramón said.

5. "You _____ have to worry," answered Raul.

6. "I need to buy some film, but I _____ know where to get it," Raul said.

7. "The supermarket _____ sell film any more," he went on.

8. "_____ the drugstore carry film?" Ramón asked.

9. "The drugstore _____ have the right kind," Raul said.

10. "Then I _____ know what to suggest," Ramón replied.

Name _____

Extra Practice

Lesson 27 Circle a word in ( ) to complete each sentence correctly.

1. "I'm writing (a/an) report about whales," Raj told Sujay on the phone.

2. "I have (a/an) article about whales that I could lend you," said Sujay.

3. "May I come over to your house in (a/an) hour to pick it up?" Raj asked.

4. "I have (a/an) swimming class until 4:30, so come by at 5:00," answered Sujay.

5. Raj ate (a/an) apple on the way to the library.

6. When Raj got back from the library, there was (a/an) message for him by the phone.

7. It said that Sujay had had (a/an) accident at his swimming class.

8. Raj called Sujay and asked, "Was it (a/an) serious accident?"

9. "I just scraped my knee, and now I've got (a/an) ice pack on it," Sujay said.

10. "I'll bring you (a/an) old comic book to look at while you're resting," Raj offered.

Lesson 28 Write *whose* or *who's* to complete each sentence correctly. Remember to capitalize the first word in a sentence or a direct quotation.

1. Min asked, "_____ coming with me to get a gift for Mrs. Wu's birthday?"

2. Linda, _____ older brother had a car, said, "Maybe my brother can drive us."

3. Bo, _____ bicycle had a basket on the handlebars, said, "We could carry the present on my bike."

4. "_____ going to pay for the present?" asked Linda.

5. "We can all chip in," said Min. "_____ hat is this?"

6. Bo, _____ uncle had given him the hat, said, "It's mine. Why do you need it?"

7. "I need it to collect contributions," answered Min. "_____ going to contribute to Mrs. Wu's birthday present?"

8. Someone asked, "_____ going to decide what to buy?"

9. "Let's vote," said Min. "The person _____ idea gets the most votes wins."

10. "_____ idea was this?" Mrs. Wu asked, smiling when they gave her the gift.

Name _____

Lesson 29 Circle a word in ( ) to correctly complete each sentence.

1. "I'm going (two/too/to) the beach today with my family," Shelley said to Claudia.

2. "Do you want to come, (two/too/to)?"

3. "I couldn't leave for another (two/too/to) hours," answered Claudia.

4. "I have (two/too/to) much to do to leave any earlier," she continued.

5. "Are you going (two/too/to) Dillon Beach?"

6. "My mom wants to go to Stinson Beach, but my father thinks that's (two/too/to) far to drive," answered Shelley.

7. "Are your sisters coming, (two/too/to)?" asked Claudia.

8. "My (two/too/to) older sisters are, but my little sister is at home with a babysitter."

9. "I'll bring a beach umbrella, in case it gets (two/too/to) hot," Claudia said.

10. "We're not going (two/too/to) a tropical island!" laughed Shelley.

Lesson 30 Circle a word in ( ) to correctly complete each sentence.

1. Paul (throwed/threw) his juggling pins into the air.

2. He (catched/caught) the pins every time, except when he tossed one under his leg.

3. After trying several times, Paul (throw/threw) his juggling pins to the ground.

4. "I'll never (catch/caught) that last pin!" he thought.

5. Roy (threw/throwed) the pin back to him and said, "Try again."

6. "Here, (caught/catch) this," Roy said as he tossed another pin to Paul.

7. Paul (catched/caught) the second pin.

8. After Paul had (thrown/threw) the pins up into the air several times to warm up, he tried the trick again.

9. "You almost (catched/caught) it that time, but the pin hit your leg," Roy said.

10. Paul tried it again, and at last (caught/catched) the third pin!

Extra Practice

Lesson 31 Write the subject pronoun that could replace the boldfaced word or words. If the pronoun would be the first word in a sentence, capitalize it.

1. **Toby and I** are looking for a record store. _____

2. **The store** has moved to a new location. _____

3. **Toby and I** looked up the new address in the phone book. _____

4. **Toby and his family** used to live in the neighborhood, so Toby knows it well. _____

5. Still, **Toby and I** seem to be lost. _____

6. **Toby** asks a woman for directions. _____

7. **The woman** points to a large warehouse across the street. _____

8. **The warehouse** looks empty. _____

9. Then **Toby** sees a line of people behind the building. _____

10. **The people** are all waiting to go inside the huge new record store. _____

Lesson 32 Choose an object pronoun from the word bank to take the place of each underlined word or phrase. Write it on the line.

me	you	her	us	him	them	it

1. Mr. Li taught <u>Julia and Ben</u> how to paint a mural. _____

2. "You can plan <u>the scene</u> before painting," Mr. Li said. _____

3. "First draw <u>a sketch</u>," he suggested. _____

4. Mr. Li gave <u>Julia and Ben</u> some blank paper. _____

5. Julia asked <u>Ben</u> to pass a pencil. _____

6. Julia described her idea to <u>Mr. Li and Ben</u>. _____

7. She asked <u>Ben</u> to create a sketch of the ocean. _____

8. Julia told <u>Mr. Li</u> they were ready to start painting. _____

9. "What color do you think we should use first?" Ben asked <u>Julia</u>. _____

10. Ben told <u>Julia</u> to use blue. _____

Name _____

Lesson 33 Circle the correct pronoun to complete each sentence. Label the pronoun *S* for *subject pronoun* or *O* for *object pronoun*.

1. Maiko, Robert, Scott, and (I/me) put on a backyard circus. ___

2. "(You/Him) and Robert can be clowns," Maiko said. ___

3. Scott helped make funny costumes for him and (me/I). ___

4. (He/Him) and I looked great in our clown suits. ___

5. "You and (I/me) can do acrobatic tricks," Scott said to Maiko. ___

6. (He/Him) and Maiko did some fancy somersaults. ___

7. Robert and (I/me) had fun performing. ___

8. I think the audience liked him and (me/I) the best. ___

9. "You and (me/I) were pretty good acrobats," Maiko told Scott. ___

10. "We and (them/they) made an excellent team!" ___

Lesson 34 Underline the correct group of words in ( ) to complete each sentence.

1. The diving instructor taught (me and David/David and me) how to snorkel.

2. (David and I/Me and David) couldn't wait to go snorkeling in the coral reef!

3. A clown fish swam past (me and David/David and me).

4. (He and I/I and he) saw a sea turtle.

5. The instructor took an underwater photo of (me and him/him and me).

6. (David and I/David and me) looked closely at a bunch of coral.

7. The instructor pointed out a rare fish to (David and I/David and me).

8. (David and I/I and David) almost stepped on a crab!

9. The crab could have pinched (me and David/David and me).

10. (Me and David/David and I) drew sketches of what we saw later that night.

Lesson 35 Circle the answer in ( ) that will complete each sentence correctly. Write the answer on the line.

1. "_____ mast holds up the sails," Steve said. (This here/This)

2. "_____ tiller in my hand steers the boat," he added. (This/This here)

3. "Take one of _____ lifejackets piled here," said Katia. (these here/these)

4. "Do you see _____ sailboats across the bay?" Steve asked. (these/those)

5. "No, _____ binoculars I'm holding are fogged up," said Jorge. (these/those)

6. "The clouds overhead are thin, but _____ clouds to the east look like they will bring rain," I said. (those/those there)

7. "Use _____ rope I'm holding to tie the cooler down," Jorge said. (that/this)

8. "_____ beach across the bay is our destination," I said. (That/This)

9. "_____ basket next to me is full of food," Katia reminded us. (This/That)

10. "_____ shady spot over there is a good place for a picnic," Jorge said. (That there/That)

Lesson 36 Underline the correct form of each verb in parentheses.

1. I (places/place) my fingers on the keyboard.

2. The typing teacher (says/say), "Begin."

3. We (types/type) as many words as we can in one minute.

4. The students (type/types) without looking at the keys.

5. Sometimes the typing teacher (cover/covers) the keys with tape.

6. Each key (have/has) one letter on it, but the keys are not in alphabetical order.

7. We (learns/learn) the placement of the keys by heart.

8. After class we (read/reads) our paragraphs aloud.

9. Some students (use/uses) a computer to write their homework papers.

10. The typing class (helps/help) us with computer skills.

Lesson 37 Underline the word in ( ) that belongs in each sentence.

1. Snakes (is/are) cool and dry to the touch.

2. A snake's forked tongue (am/is) helpful in smelling and locating prey.

3. Some snakes (are/is) excellent hunters.

4. Snakes (were/was) in existence millions of years ago.

5. Snakes (are/is) plentiful in a variety of climates.

6. Like alligators, snakes (is/are) reptiles.

7. Rattlesnakes (is/are) very dangerous.

8. Their venom (is/are) poisonous.

9. Anacondas of South America (am/are) sometimes 30 feet long!

10. The poisonous coral snake (are/is) an especially colorful snake.

Lesson 38 Rewrite the sentences so they tell about the *past*.

1. We <u>will visit</u> the Grand Canyon. _____

2. We <u>will photograph</u> the Grand Canyon's colorful cliffs. _____
   _____

3. Jessie <u>spies</u> a wild burro in the park. _____
   _____

4. We <u>will hike</u> down into the canyon on the Bright Angel Trail. _____
   _____

5. Tom <u>looks</u> out for rattlesnakes. _____

6. A lizard <u>rests</u> near the trail. _____

7. The Wongs <u>raft</u> down the Colorado River. _____
   _____

8. They <u>will travel</u> through part of the canyon's deep gorge. _____
   _____

Name _____

Extra Practice

Lesson 39 Rewrite each sentence correctly.

1. I haven't never given no speech before. _____

2. I don't want to stand up in front of no audience. _____
   _____

3. What if I get up on stage and I'm not able to say nothing? _____
   _____

4. I don't remember none of my speech. _____

5. What if I tell a joke and the audience doesn't do nothing? _____
   _____

6. My voice doesn't never shake like this. _____

7. Don't tell nobody I'm nervous. _____

8. I hope I don't have no sneezing fit. _____

9. I'm not really scared no more. _____

10. Please don't throw no tomatoes. _____

Lesson 40 Underline the correct form of the adjective in ( ).

1. The state of Alaska is (more big/bigger) than the state of Hawaii.

2. Some folks think the landscape of Alaska is (beautifuller/more beautiful) than Hawaii.

3. Alaska is (colder/more cold) than Hawaii.

4. Hawaii is (more rainy/rainier) than Alaska.

5. Alaska became a state (sooner/more soon) than Hawaii.

6. The climate of Hawaii is (pleasanter/more pleasant) than that of Alaska.

7. The Big Island of Hawaii is (more young/younger) than the other Hawaiian islands.

8. Hawaii is a (newer/more new) landmass than Alaska.

9. The sunsets in Hawaii are (more colorful/colorfuler) than those in most other places.

10. Hawaii's landscape is rugged, but Alaska's is (more rugged/ruggeder).

Name _____

Lesson 41 Circle each capitalization and punctuation error. Then label each sentence *statement, question, command,* or *exclamation.*

1. more than 2,000 fans have bought tickets for the game today _____

2. Wow, this will be the largest crowd we've ever had _____

3. Why are so many people coming today! _____

4. it's the last game of the season _____

5. Is anybody hungry _____

6. bring me a hot dog and a lemonade _____

7. What a great play _____

8. what's the score. _____

9. Pass me the binoculars _____

10. don't spill any lemonade on them? _____

Lesson 42 Circle each capitalization error.

1. My Family went on vacation to Salt lake City, utah.

2. When we got to my aunt's house in arizona, I had a terrible Cold.

3. Aunt rose took me to the Doctor.

4. She told me that dr. Chu is a very good doctor.

5. We drove to his Office on mason Avenue.

6. On the wall in the Waiting Room, there was a poster of michael jordan.

7. I decided that Doctor Chu must be a nice Guy.

8. After my Appointment, we went to an ice cream parlor called the Spotted cow.

9. I'm glad to be Home in stillwater, oklahoma.

10. On August 15 I will start a new term at kennedy elementary school.

Extra Practice

Lesson 43 Circle each error in an abbreviation or an initial.

1. Mrs. Edith v. Morrow runs a bookstore.

2. Her store is on Appletree ave

3. I went to Mrs Morrow's store to buy the new book by my favorite author.

4. His name is t h Keene. mr Keene is a terrific writer.

5. He lives in my town on Allerton blvd. Sycamore st is my street.

6. My dentist, Dr. Janice F Silverburg, knows T.H. Keene.

7. Perhaps dr. Silverburg could ask Mr Keene to sign my book.

8. Maybe she'll introduce me to mr Keene!

Lesson 44 Rewrite each title correctly.

1. We saw the movie creatures of the deep.

   _____

2. I wanted to read a book about sharks called They aren't Just teeth.

   _____

3. My dad has a book called cooking Like papa Used to cook.

   _____

4. Dad likes to sing on Top of old smoky when he cooks.

   _____

5. I read a short story called The purple speckled box.

   _____

6. It's by the same author who wrote the book mirror behind the wall.

   _____

7. Next week we are going to see a movie called king of the saltwater eels.

   _____

8. I wrote a poem called Don't squeal If You feel an Eel.

   _____

Name _____

Lesson 45 Rewrite each set of boldfaced words as a contraction or a possessive noun.

(1) **The father of Ellen** took her to a ranch in the country to ride horses. (2) **It is** her favorite thing to do. (3) The **owner of the ranch** showed Ellen his best horses. (4) The **manes of the horses** were shiny and full. (5) "**There is** the horse I want to ride," Ellen said. (6) The **daughter of the owner** is an expert rider. (7) **The name of her horse** is Firestreak. (8) "**What is** (9) **the name of my horse**?" Ellen asked. "Its name is Peanuts. (10) **Let us** go!"

1. _____
2. _____
3. _____
4. _____
5. _____
6. _____
7. _____
8. _____
9. _____
10. _____

Lesson 46 Add commas where they belong.

1. My aunt holds block parties on her street in June July and August.
2. There's music dancing, games and food.
3. She always asks my brother, my sister, and me to help.
4. I helped serve hot dogs corn on the cob and lemonade.
5. I asked people if they liked mustard ketchup, or onions on their hot dogs.
6. One man said he liked mustard ketchup onions and pickles.
7. We made paper hats had a parade and lit sparklers on the Fourth of July.
8. We decorated our bikes with red white, and blue streamers for the parade.
9. We put on bathing suits, turned on the sprinkler, and ran through the water.
10. Then we sat on my aunt's porch fanned ourselves and swatted mosquitoes.

Lesson 47 Add *Yes, No, Well,* or someone's name to the beginning of each sentence. Be sure to use commas correctly.

1. _____ can you blow a bubble with your bubble gum?

2. _____ I can blow the biggest bubble you've ever seen!

3. _____ it's not hard to do.

4. _____ please give me a piece of bubble gum.

5. _____ do you want to have a bubble-blowing contest?

6. _____ I'm not sure if I can blow a bubble at all.

7. _____ I've never tried.

8. _____ this is your big chance.

9. _____ you're right. Give me a piece of gum.

10. _____ look at the bubble you blew!

Lesson 48 Write *C* next to each compound sentence. Add missing commas to the compound sentences.

1. I wanted to play on the soccer team but my brother said I was too small. ____

2. I'm a good kicker. ____

3. I set up a goal in the backyard and I began to practice. ____

4. The tryouts are in the fall and I am going to be ready for them. ____

5. Every morning I run laps around the block. ____

6. In the afternoons I practice shooting goals. ____

7. I am tired at the end of the day. ____

8. Every weekend the kids in my neighborhood go to the roller rink and they skate for hours. ____

9. I love to roller skate but this summer I trained for soccer instead. ____

10. I will try out for the soccer team next month and I will surprise everyone! ____

Name _____

Lesson 49 Add quotation marks to the direct quotations. Draw a star next to the indirect quotations.

1. This is my favorite painting, said the artist. ____

2. He told us that it had taken him two years to finish. ____

3. First I decided on the colors, and then I thought about shapes, he said. ____

4. Sometimes the colors are more important than the shapes, he added. ____

5. He asked, Do you have any questions? ____

6. George asked, What were you thinking about when you painted this one? ____

7. The artist said, I was thinking about my childhood home in Clarksdale, Mississippi. ____

8. He said that most of his paintings were of things he remembered from his childhood. ____

9. Naomi asked, How long have you been an artist? ____

10. The artist said that he began to paint when he was three years old. ____

Lesson 50 Add the missing punctuation marks to each sentence.

1. The scout leader said We are going on a fishing trip at the end of the month.

2. I asked Where are we going?

3. She said We are going to Sandy Point Lake.

4. Are we going to go out in rowboats Scarlet asked.

5. The scout leader said Yes, we are going to rent rowboats.

6. Everyone will be able to fish she said.

7. Carla asked How long will we be gone?

8. The scout leader said We will leave at 4 A.M. and return about 8 P.M.

9. She said Have your parents sign these permission slips.

10. I'll take mine home today I said.

Name _____

G.U.M.

Choose the answer that describes the underlined part of each sentence. Fill in the circle next to each of your answers.

1. Liliuokalani <u>was the last queen of Hawaii</u>.
   - (a) complete subject
   - (b) complete predicate

2. <u>This Hawaiian queen</u> reigned from 1891 to 1893.
   - (a) simple subject
   - (b) complete subject

3. Hawaii <u>was</u> an independent kingdom.
   - (a) simple subject
   - (b) simple predicate

4. Many <u>settlers</u> wanted United States statehood for the islands.
   - (a) simple subject
   - (b) simple predicate

5. The settlers <u>rebelled</u> against the queen.
   - (a) simple subject
   - (b) simple predicate

6. She <u>lost</u> her throne.
   - (a) simple subject
   - (b) simple predicate

7. <u>Hawaii</u> became a state in 1959.
   - (a) simple subject
   - (b) simple predicate

8. Liliuokalani wrote an <u>autobiography</u>.
   - (a) direct object
   - (b) simple predicate

9. She also wrote a famous <u>song</u>.
   - (a) prepositional phrase
   - (b) direct object

10. "Aloha Oe" is often played <u>on the ukulele</u>.
    - (a) prepositional phrase
    - (b) complete predicate

11. The governor of the state of Hawaii lives <u>in Liliuokalani's old house</u>.
    - (a) complete predicate
    - (b) prepositional phrase

12. Hawaiian students learn <u>about the last queen</u>.
    - (a) complete predicate
    - (b) prepositional phrase

Choose the sentence that says more. Fill in the circle next to your answer.

13. (a) Lech Walesa led a movement for workers' rights in Poland.

    (b) Lech Walesa is an important leader.

14. (a) People supported Lech Walesa.

    (b) Walesa was elected president of Poland in 1990.

Read each group of words. Fill in the circle next to the answer that describes that group of words.

15. Winston Churchill, a very great leader.
    (a) sentence fragment   (b) run-on

16. Led the British during World War II.
    (a) sentence fragment   (b) compound sentence

17. Became Prime Minister in 1940.
    (a) run-on   (b) sentence fragment

18. Churchill stuttered as a boy, but he later became famous for his moving speeches.
    (a) run-on   (b) compound sentence

19. He encouraged the British in hard times, and they loved him.
    (a) run-on   (b) compound sentence

20. German planes bombed London, Churchill cried when he saw the damage.
    (a) compound sentence   (b) comma splice

21. The British fought hard during World War II they never surrendered.
    (a) fragment   (b) run-on

Choose the correct end mark for each sentence. Fill in the circle next to your answer.

22. What makes a great leader__   (a) .   (b) ?   (c) !

23. Leadership takes courage and determination__   (a) .   (b) ?   (c) !

24. Please help me with my campaign for class president__   (a) .   (b) ?   (c) !

25. Hooray, I won the election__   (a) .   (b) ?   (c) !

Decide which boldfaced word is a noun. Fill in the circle with the letter that matches it.

1. Our class **adopted** a pair of **canaries**.   ⓐ   ⓑ
   a   b

2. Their **feathers** are **bright** yellow.   ⓐ   ⓑ
   a   b

3. **Sometimes** they sing during **class**.   ⓐ   ⓑ
   a   b

Decide what kind of word the boldfaced word is. Fill in the circle next to your answer.

4. Last summer my family went to three national **parks**.
   ⓐ singular noun   ⓑ plural noun

5. We took our **dog** Rufus with us.
   ⓐ singular noun   ⓑ plural noun

6. Each night we slept in a different **campground**.
   ⓐ proper noun   ⓑ common noun

7. My favorite place was the **Grand Canyon**.
   ⓐ proper noun   ⓑ common noun

8. It is located in **Arizona**.
   ⓐ proper noun   ⓑ common noun

9. We rode down the canyon **on** mules.
   ⓐ preposition   ⓑ pronoun

10. We camped **beside** a stream.
    ⓐ pronoun   ⓑ preposition

11. **Who** bought a pet on the way home?
    ⓐ possessive pronoun   ⓑ interrogative pronoun

12. Hannah bought **her** hamster. She named him Bear.
    ⓐ possessive pronoun   ⓑ interrogative pronoun

13. Bear performs tricks all day in **his** cage.
    ⓐ possessive pronoun   ⓑ interrogative pronoun

14. Sometimes **he** runs all night on his wheel.
    ⓐ possessive pronoun   ⓑ personal pronoun

Choose the best word to complete each sentence. Fill in the circle next to your answer.

15. Some birds have wings, _____ they can't fly.
    (a) and   (b) but   (c) or

16. The kiwi has short legs, _____ its feathers are brown and shaggy.
    (a) and   (b) but   (c) or

17. People seldom see kiwi birds because they run away _____ because they are already hiding.
    (a) and   (b) but   (c) or

18. Birds _____ can't smell very well, but kiwis can.
    (a) usual   (b) usually

19. The kiwi looks for food in wet, _____ forests.
    (a) thick   (b) thickly

Decide whether the boldfaced word is an action verb or a linking verb. Fill in the circle next to your answer.

20. Kiwi **is** a kind of fruit as well as a kind of bird.
    (a) action verb   (b) linking verb

21. People **make** ice cream and pies with kiwi fruit.
    (a) action verb   (b) linking verb

22. My aunt **eats** kiwi fruit on yogurt.
    (a) action verb   (b) linking verb

Decide whether the boldfaced word is a main verb or a helping verb. Fill in the circle next to your answer.

23. Kiwi fruit is **grown** in China, France, and Japan.
    (a) main verb   (b) helping verb

24. The center of a kiwi fruit is **filled** with black seeds.
    (a) main verb   (b) helping verb

25. You **can** eat the kiwi seeds.
    (a) main verb   (b) helping verb

Find the correct word to complete each sentence. Fill in the circle next to that word.

1. Do you have _____ raincoat?
   (a) your   (b) you're

2. _____ going to need it today.
   (a) Your   (b) You're

3. I hope you brought _____ rain boots, too.
   (a) your   (b) you're

4. Put the thermometers over _____.
   (a) their   (b) there   (c) they're

5. _____ for our science experiment.
   (a) Their   (b) They're   (c) There

6. Do the students have _____ notebooks?
   (a) their   (b) there   (c) they're

7. _____ going to need pencils, too.
   (a) They're   (b) Their   (c) there

8. _____ extremely windy today.
   (a) Its   (b) It's

9. That sign fell on _____ side!
   (a) its   (b) it's

10. _____ going to be repaired tomorrow.
    (a) Its   (b) It's

11. It has snowed for _____ whole hour.
    (a) a   (b) an

12. Can you measure the snowfall with _____ ruler?
    (a) a   (b) an

13. Mrs. Ingalls read a _____ story about a tornado.
    (a) good   (b) well

14. She reads _____.
    (a) good   (b) well

Name _____

Decide which word belongs in each sentence. Fill in the circle next to your answer.

15. All of Mr. Williams's talks _____ interesting.
    - (a) are
    - (b) is

16. Last week his talk _____ about blizzards.
    - (a) was
    - (b) were

17. All of my classmates _____ fascinated.
    - (a) was
    - (b) were

18. I _____ know what causes blizzards.
    - (a) don't
    - (b) doesn't

19. Randy _____ know, either.
    - (a) don't
    - (b) doesn't

20. _____ read the book *White Fang,* by Jack London?
    - (a) Whose
    - (b) Who's

21. _____ copy of *White Fang* is this?
    - (a) Whose
    - (b) Who's

22. I like Jack London, _____.
    - (a) too
    - (b) two
    - (c) to

23. I have read _____ of his books about life in the Arctic.
    - (a) too
    - (b) two
    - (c) to

24. I _____ a cold after reading a book about being lost in the snow.
    - (a) catch
    - (b) caught

25. My brother had _____ the book on the sofa for me to read.
    - (a) threw
    - (b) thrown

Choose the correct word or phrase to complete each sentence. Fill in the circle next to your answer.

1. _____ book in my hand says that there are 132 rooms in the White House!
   (a) That   (b) This

2. _____ room is called the Blue Room.
   (a) That there   (b) That

3. _____ chairs over there were chosen by President James Monroe.
   (a) These   (b) Those

4. _____ wanted to take a tour of the Pentagon in Arlington, Virginia.
   (a) Me and Mario (b) Mario and I

5. A guard told _____ that the Pentagon is a high-security building.
   (a) Mario and I   (b) Mario and me

6. The Bureau of Engraving and Printing _____ in Washington, D.C.
   (a) are   (b) is

7. Huge machines _____ the nation's paper money there.
   (a) print   (b) prints

8. No, they don't _____ visitors money as a souvenir.
   (a) gives   (b) give

9. The Capitol building and the National Gallery _____ in Washington, D.C.
   (a) are   (b) is

10. The French engineer Pierre L'Enfant _____ Washington's first city planner.
    (a) were   (b) was

11. _____ picture shows L'Enfant's earliest plans.
    (a) This   (b) This here

12. _____ spot is where the Capitol building was constructed.
    (a) That there   (b) That

13. When I visited the Capitol building, I _____ more than a dozen photographs.
    (a) take   (b) took

14. Is the White House _____ than the Capitol building?
    (a) more large   (b) larger

15. No, but I think the White House is _____.
    (a) more elegant (b) eleganter

Name _____

Choose the correct pronoun to replace each boldfaced word or phrase. Fill in the circle next to your answer.

16. **Ira and Kate** visited Washington, D.C.
    (a) It   (b) She   (c) We   (d) They

17. **Kate** wanted to see the Lincoln Memorial.
    (a) He   (b) She   (c) It   (d) We

18. Ira gave a book about Abraham Lincoln to **Kate**.
    (a) her   (b) it   (c) them   (d) she

19. Kate read **the book** on the airplane.
    (a) her   (b) him   (c) them   (d) it

20. Did Bill and **Kate** tour the White House?
    (a) her   (b) them   (c) she   (d) they

21. A guard told Bill and **Kate** to stay with the group.
    (a) her   (b) them   (c) she   (d) it

Decide which sentence in each pair uses negative words correctly. Fill in the circle next to the correct sentence.

22. (a) Washington, D.C., isn't no state.

    (b) Washington, D.C., isn't a state.

23. (a) Washington D.C.'s founders didn't want to build the nation's capital in no particular state.

    (b) Washington D.C.'s founders didn't want to build the nation's capital in any particular state.

24. (a) They couldn't come up with a solution until Alexander Hamilton suggested building the Capitol on federal land.

    (b) They couldn't come up with no solution until Alexander Hamilton suggested building the Capitol on federal land.

25. (a) Federal land doesn't belong to a state.

    (b) Federal land doesn't belong to no state.

Read each sentence and choose the correct end mark. Fill in the circle next to your answer.

1. Oh, no, the screen went blank___   (a) ?   (b) .   (c) !

2. What should I do now___   (a) ?   (b) .   (c) !

3. Please start up the computer again___   (a) ?   (b) .   (c) !

Decide which boldfaced word needs to be capitalized. Fill in the circle with the letter that matches it.

4. **computers** have counted votes in U.S. **elections** since 1952.   (a)   (b)
   a   b

5. That **year** Eisenhower ran for President against **stevenson**.   (a)   (b)
   a   b

6. The **computer** predicted that **president** Eisenhower would win.   (a)   (b)
   a   b

7. I read a book called <u>**what** Computers Can Do **for** You</u>.   (a)   (b)
            a   b

8. <u>Caught **in** the **net**</u> is a movie about the Internet.   (a)   (b)
      a   b

Choose the answer that shows the correct way to shorten the underlined part of the sentence. Fill in the circle next to your answer.

9. <u>Mister Paul Simon</u> Colella is a computer programmer.
   (a) M'r Paul S   (b) Mr. Paul S.

10. His office is on Elm <u>Street</u>.
    (a) str.   (b) St.

11. <u>Do not</u> use a disk without checking it for computer viruses.
    (a) Don't   (b) Dont'

12. A virus can damage <u>the files on a computer</u>.
    (a) a computer's files   (b) a computers' files

13. <u>The computers of these students</u> have programs that scan for viruses.
    (a) These student's computers   (b) These students' computers

14. <u>They are</u> checked every day for new viruses.
    (a) Theyre   (b) They're

Name _____

171

G.U.M.

Decide where the comma belongs in each sentence. Fill in the circle with the matching letter.

15. Maya did you save your picture on the computer?   (a) (b)
     a   b

16. No I decided not to save it.   (a) (b)
     a b

17. I tried out a music program a paint program, and a virtual reality game. (a) (b)
          a   b

18. I ran, swam and flew in virtual reality.   (a) (b)
          a   b

19. Computers were bigger fifty years ago but they were less powerful.   (a) (b)
                            a   b

20. My dad has never used a computer but I will teach him.   (a) (b)
               a   b

Decide whether each sentence is missing quotation marks or is correct as written. Fill in the circle next to your answer.

21. Wow, look at this photo of pigs flying! said Alicia.
     (a) missing quotation marks   (b) correct as written

22. Sarah said that she knew how the photo was made.
     (a) missing quotation marks   (b) correct as written

Choose the punctuation that belongs in the blank to complete the sentence correctly. Fill in the circle next to your answer.

23. "An artist copies photos of a pig, a bird's wings, and the sky into a computer___ explained Sarah.
     (a) ,"   (b) "

24. "What happens next___ Mira asked.
     (a) ,"   (b) ?"

25. Sarah said___ "The computer combines the photos any way the artist wants."
     (a) "   (b) ,

Language Handbook Table of Contents

Name _____

Mechanics

Section 1 Capitalization

- **Capitalize the first word in a sentence.**
  The kangaroo rat is an amazing animal.

- **Capitalize people's names and the names of particular places.**
  Gregory Gordon   Washington Monument

- **Capitalize titles of respect.**
  Mr. Alvarez   Dr. Chin   Ms. Murphy

- **Capitalize family titles used just before people's names and titles of respect that are part of names.**
  Uncle Frank   Aunt Mary   Governor Adamson

- **Capitalize initials of names.**
  Thomas Paul Gerard (T.P. Gerard)

- **Capitalize place names and words formed from them.**
  France   French   China   Chinese

- **Capitalize the months of the year and the days of the week.**
  February   April   Monday   Tuesday

- **Capitalize important words in the names of groups.**
  American Lung Association   Veterans of Foreign Wars

- **Capitalize important words in the names of holidays.**
  Veterans Day   Fourth of July

- **Capitalize the first word in the greeting or closing of a letter.**
  Dear Edmundo,   Yours truly,

- **Capitalize the word *I*.**
  Frances and I watched the movie together.

- **Capitalize the first, last, and most important words in a title. Be sure to capitalize all verbs including *is* and *was*.**
  Island of the Blue Dolphins
  Always Is a Strange Place to Be

- **Capitalize the first word in a direct quotation.**
  Aunt Rose said, "Please pass the clam dip."

Section 2 Abbreviations and Initials

Abbreviations are shortened forms of words. Many abbreviations begin with a capital letter and end with a period.

- **You can abbreviate titles of address when you write.**
  Mister (Mr. Brian Davis)   Mistress (Mrs. Maria Rosario)
  Doctor (Dr. Emily Chu)   Junior (Everett Castle, Jr.)
  Note: *Ms.* is a title of address used for women. It is not an abbreviation, but it requires a period (Ms. Anita Brown).

- **You can abbreviate words used in addresses when you write.**
  Street (St.)   Avenue (Ave.)   Route (Rte.)   Boulevard (Blvd.)   Road (Rd.)

- **You can abbreviate days of the week when you take notes.**
  Sunday (Sun.)   Wednesday (Wed.)   Friday (Fri.)
  Monday (Mon.)   Thursday (Thurs.)   Saturday (Sat.)
  Tuesday (Tues.)

- **You can abbreviate months of the year when you take notes.**
  January (Jan.)   April (Apr.)   October (Oct.)
  February (Feb.)   August (Aug.)   November (Nov.)
  March (Mar.)   September (Sept.)   December (Dec.)
  (May, June, and July do not have abbreviated forms.)

- **You can abbreviate directions when you take notes.**
  North (N)   East (E)   South (S)   West (W)

An *initial* is the first letter of a name. An initial is written as a capital letter and a period. Sometimes initials are used for the names of countries or cities.

Michael Paul Sanders (M.P. Sanders)   United States of America (U.S.A.)
Washington, District of Columbia (Washington, D.C.)

Section 3 Titles

- **Underline titles of books, newspapers, TV series, movies, and magazines.**
  <u>Island of the Blue Dolphins</u>   <u>Miami Herald</u>   <u>I Love Lucy</u>
  Note: These titles are put in italics when using a word processor.

- **Use quotation marks around articles in magazines, short stories, chapters in books, songs, and poems.**
  "This Land Is Your Land"   "The Gift"   "Eletelephony"

- **Capitalize the first, last, and most important words. Be sure to capitalize all verbs, including *is* and *was*.**
  A Knight in the Attic   *My Brother Sam Is Dead*

Section 4 Quotation Marks

- Put quotation marks (" ") around the titles of articles, magazines, short stories, book chapters, songs, and poems.

  My favorite short story is "Revenge of the Reptiles."

- Put quotation marks around a *direct quotation*, or a speaker's exact words.

  "Did you see that alligator?" Max asked.

Writing a Conversation

- Quotation marks are used to separate a speaker's exact words from the rest of the sentence. Begin a direct quotation with a capital letter. Use a comma to separate the direct quotation from the speaker's name.

  Rory said, "There are no alligators in this area."

- When a direct quotation comes at the end of a sentence, put the end mark inside the last quotation mark.

  Max cried, "Look out!"

- When writing a conversation, begin a new paragraph with each change of speaker.

  Rory and Max leaped away from the pond. Max panted, "I swear I saw a huge, scaly tail and a flat snout in the water!"

  "Relax," Rory said. "I told you there are no alligators around here."

Section 5 Spelling

Use these tips if you are not sure how to spell a word you want to write:

- Think of a word you know that rhymes with the word you want to spell. Or think of a word you know that has parts that sound like the word you're spelling. Word parts that sound alike are often spelled the same.
  Spell rhymes with *well.*
  If you can spell *cat* and *log,* you can spell *catalog.*

- Say the word aloud and break it into parts, or syllables. Try spelling each word part. Put the parts together to spell the whole word.

- Write the word. Make sure there is a vowel in every syllable. If the word looks wrong to you, try spelling it other ways.

Correct spelling helps readers understand what you write. Use a dictionary to check the spellings of any words you are not sure about.

Section 6 End Marks

Every sentence must end with a period, an exclamation point, or a question mark.

- Use a *period* at the end of a statement or a command.
  My grandfather and I look alike. (*statement*)
  Step back very slowly. (*command*)

- Use an *exclamation point* at the end of a firm command or at the end of a sentence that shows great feeling or excitement.
  Get away from the cliff! (*command*)
  What an incredible sight! (*exclamation*)

- Use a *question mark* at the end of an asking sentence.
  How many miles is it to Tucson? (*question*)

Section 7 Apostrophes

An apostrophe (') is used to form the possessive of a noun or to join two words in a contraction.

- **Possessives show ownership. To make a singular noun into a possessive, add an apostrophe and *s*.**
  The bike belongs to Carmen. It is Carmen's bike.
  The truck belongs to Mr. Ross. It is Mr. Ross's truck.

- **To form a possessive from a plural noun that ends in *s*, add only an apostrophe.**
  Those books belong to my sisters. They are my sisters' books.
  Two families own this house. It is the families' vacation spot.

- **Some plural nouns do not end in *s*. To form possessives with these nouns, add an apostrophe and *s*.**
  The women own those boats. They are the women's boats.
  The children left their boots here. The children's boots are wet.

- **Use an apostrophe to replace the dropped letters in a contraction.**
  couldn't (could n**o**t)   it's (it **is**)
  didn't (did n**o**t)   I'm (I **am**)
  hasn't (has n**o**t)   they'll (they **wi**ll)

Commas in Sentences

- **Use a comma after an introductory word in a sentence.**
  Yes, I'd love to go to the movies.
  Actually, we had a great time.

- **Use a comma to separate items in a series.**
  We ate cheese, bread, and fruit.
  The puppy whined, scratched at the door, and then barked loudly.

- **Use a comma when speaking directly to a person.**
  Akila, will you please stand up?
  We would like you to sing, Akila.

- **Use a comma to separate a direct quotation from the speaker's name.**
  Harold asked, "How long do I have to sit here?"
  "You must sit there until Anton returns," Vic said.

- **Use a comma with the joining words *and*, *or*, or *but* when combining two sentences.**
  Lisa liked the reptiles best, but Lyle preferred the amphibians.

Commas in Letters

- **Use a comma after the greeting and closing of a friendly letter.**
  Dear Reginald,   Your friend, Deke

Commas with Dates and Place Names

- **Use a comma to separate the month and the day from the year.**
  We clinched the pennant on September 8, 1996.

- **Use a comma to separate the day from the date.**
  It was Sunday, November 5.

- **Use a comma to separate the name of a city or town from the name of a state.**
  I visited Memphis, Tennessee.

Sentence Structure and Parts of Speech

Section 9 The Sentence

A *sentence* is a group of words that tells a complete thought. A sentence has two parts: a *subject* and a *predicate*.

- The subject tells *whom* or *what*.
  <u>The swimmers</u> race.

- The predicate tells *what happened*.
  The judges <u>watch carefully</u>.

There are four kinds of sentences: *statement, question, command,* and *exclamation.*

- A sentence that tells something is called a *telling sentence* or *statement.* It is also called a *declarative sentence.* A statement ends with a period.
  Jake swam faster than anyone.

- A sentence that asks something is called an *asking sentence* or *question.* It is also called an *interrogative sentence.* A question ends with a question mark.
  Did Sammy qualify for the finals?

- A sentence that tells someone to do something is called a *command.* A command usually ends with a period, but a firm command can end with an exclamation point.
  Keep your eyes on the finish line.
  Watch out for that bee!

- A sentence that shows excitement or surprise is called an *exclamation.* An exclamation ends with an exclamation point.
  Jake has won the race!

Section 10 Subjects

The *subject* of a sentence tells whom or what the sentence is about.

- A sentence can have one subject.
  <u>Mary</u> wrote a book.

- A sentence can have more than one subject.
  <u>Alex and Mark</u> have already read the book.

The *complete subject* includes all the words that name and tell about the subject.
  <u>Many different students</u> have borrowed the book.

The *simple subject* is the most important word or words in the complete subject.
  Many different <u>students</u> have borrowed the book.

Note: Sometimes the simple subject and the complete subject are the same.
  <u>Ricardo</u> is writing a book about robots.

Section 11 Predicates

The *predicate* of a sentence tells what happened.

The *complete predicate* includes a verb and all the words that tell what happened.

- A complete predicate can tell what the subject of the sentence did. This kind of predicate includes an action verb.
  Mary <u>won an award</u>.

- A complete predicate can also tell more about the subject. This kind of predicate includes a linking verb.
  Mary <u>is a talented writer</u>.

A *compound predicate* is two or more predicates that share the same subject. Compound predicates are often connected by the joining word *and* or *or*.

Ramon <u>sang and danced</u> in the play. Mary <u>wrote the play and directed it</u>.

The *simple predicate* is the most important word or words in the complete predicate. The simple predicate is always a verb.

Mary <u>won</u> an award for her performance.
She <u>will receive</u> a trophy next week.

Section 12 Simple and Compound Sentences

A *simple sentence* tells one complete thought.

Arthur has a rock collection.

A *compound sentence* is made up of two simple sentences joined by the word *and*, *or*, or *but*. Two simple sentences can go together to make one compound sentence if the ideas in the simple sentences are related.

Arthur has a rock collection<u>, and</u> Mary collects shells.

Section 13 Fragments, Run-ons, and Comma Splices

A *fragment* is not a sentence because it is missing a subject or a predicate.

- Fragments are also called *incomplete sentences* because they do not tell a complete thought.
  Sumi and Ali. (*missing a predicate that tells what happened*)
  Went hiking in the woods. (*missing a subject that tells who*)

A *run-on sentence* is two complete sentences that are run together.

Sumi went hiking Ali went swimming.

- To fix a run-on sentence, use a comma and *and*, *or*, or *but* to join the two complete sentences.
  Sumi went hiking<u>, but</u> Ali went swimming.

A *comma splice* is two complete sentences that have a comma between them but are missing a joining word such as *and, or,* or *but.*

> Sumi went hiking yesterday, Ali went swimming.

- **To fix a comma splice, add *and, or,* or *but* after the comma.**

> Sumi went hiking yesterday, **and** Ali went swimming.

Try not to string too many short sentences together when you write. Instead, combine sentences and take out unnecessary information.

> **Incorrect:** I stared at him and he stared at me and I told him to go away and he wouldn't so then I called my big sister.
> **Correct:** We stared at each other. I asked him to go away, but he wouldn't. Then I called my big sister.

Section 14 Nouns

A *common noun* names any person, place, or thing.

> Ira visited an auto **museum** with his **friends**. They saw old **cars** there.

A *proper noun* names a certain person, place, or thing. Proper nouns begin with a capital letter.

> **Ira** wants to visit the **Sonoran Desert** in **Mexico**.

Section 15 Adjectives

An *adjective* is a word that tells more about a noun.

- **Some adjectives tell what kind.**
  Jim observed the **huge** elephant. The **enormous** beast towered above him.

- **Some adjectives tell how many.**
  The elephant was **twelve** feet tall. It weighed **several** tons.

- **Sometimes an adjective follows the noun it describes.**
  Jim was **careful** not to anger the elephant. The elephant was **frightening**. Jim was **happy** when the trainer led it away.

- **Some adjectives tell which one. The words *this, that, these,* and *those* can be used as adjectives. Use *this* and *these* to talk about things that are nearby. Use *that* and *those* to talk about things that are far away.**

  This book is about rhinos.
  That rhino is enormous!
  These rhinos just came to the zoo.
  Those funny-looking creatures are wildebeests.
  Note: Never use *here* or *there* after the adjectives *this, that, these,* and *those.*
  Incorrect: **That there** wildebeest is running fast.
  Correct: **That** baby zebra has wandered away from its mother.

Section 16 Pronouns

A *pronoun* can replace a noun naming a person, place, or thing. Pronouns include *I, me, you, we, us, he, she, it, they,* and *them.*

- **A pronoun may take the place of the subject of a sentence. Do not use both the pronoun and the noun it replaces together.**
  Incorrect: Rita is an excellent hockey player. <u>**Rita she**</u> made the team.
  Correct: Rita plays goalie. <u>**She**</u> never lets the other team score.

- **A pronoun may replace a noun that is the direct object of a verb.**
  Rita's team played the Bobcats. Rita's team beat <u>**them**</u>.

- **A pronoun must match the noun it replaces. A singular pronoun must be used in place of a singular noun.**
  Nick saved the game. <u>**He**</u> kicked a goal at the last minute.

- **A plural pronoun must be used in place of a plural noun.**
  The Bobcats were upset. <u>**They**</u> had not lost a game all season.

- *This, that, these,* and *those* **can be used as demonstrative pronouns. Use** *this* **and** *these* **to talk about one or more things that are nearby. Use** *that* **and** *those* **to talk about one or more things that are far away.**
  <u>**This**</u> is a soft rug.
  <u>**These**</u> are sweeter than those over there.
  <u>**That**</u> is where I sat yesterday.
  <u>**Those**</u> are new chairs.

- **Possessive pronouns show ownership. The words** *my, your, his, her, its, their,* **and** *our* **are possessive pronouns.**
  Those skates belong to my brother. Those are <u>**his**</u> kneepads, too.

- **The interrogative pronouns** *who, what,* **and** *which* **are used to ask questions.**
  <u>**Who**</u> has brought the volleyball?   <u>**What**</u> is a wicket used for?
  <u>**Which**</u> net is used for volleyball?

Section 17 Verbs

An *action verb* shows action in a sentence.
Scientists <u>**study**</u> the natural world.
They <u>**learn**</u> how the laws of nature work.

- **Sometimes a** *helping verb* **is needed to help the main verb show action. A helping verb comes before a main verb.**
  Some scientists <u>**are**</u> studying the glaciers of Antarctica.
  These studies <u>**will**</u> help scientists learn about Earth's history.

- **Verbs can tell about the** *present,* **the** *past,* **or the** *future.*
  Few people <u>**travel**</u> in Antarctica. (*present tense*)
  Explorers first <u>**traveled**</u> to the South Pole over 100 years ago. (*past tense*)
  Other explorers <u>**will travel**</u> to the South Pole in the future. (*future tense*)

- To show past action, *-ed* is added to most verbs. Verbs that do not add *-ed* are called *irregular verbs*. Here are some common irregular verbs.

Present	Past	With *have, has,* or *had*
bring	brought	brought
catch	caught	caught
come	came	come
give	gave	given
go	went	gone
sing	sang	sung
sleep	slept	slept
take	took	taken
throw	threw	thrown

- The subject and its verb must agree. Add *s* or *es* to a verb in the present tense when the subject is a singular noun or *he, she,* or *it.* Do not add *s* if the subject is a plural noun or if the subject is *I, you, we,* or *they.*
  An Antarctic explorer needs special equipment.
  (*singular subject:* **An Antarctic explorer;** *verb + s or es:* **needs**)
  Explorers carry climbing tools and survival gear.
  (*plural subject:* **Explorers;** *verb without s or es:* **carry**)
  I like stories about Antarctica.
  (*subject:* **I;** *verb without s or es:* **like**)

A *linking verb* does not show action. It connects the subject of a sentence to a word or words in the predicate that tell about the subject. Linking verbs include *am, is, are, was,* and *were. Seem* and *become* are linking verbs, too.

Explorers <u>are</u> brave. That route <u>seems</u> very long and dangerous.

Section 18 Adverbs

An *adverb* is usually used to describe a verb.

- **Many adverbs end in *-ly.***
  Andrew approached the snake cage <u>slowly</u>. He <u>cautiously</u> peered inside.

- **Some adverbs do not end in *-ly.***
  Andrew knew that snakes can move <u>fast</u>.

- *Very* is an adverb meaning "to a high degree" or "extremely." Never use *real* in place of *very.*

Incorrect	Correct
The snake's fangs were <u>real</u> sharp.	The snake's fangs were <u>very</u> sharp.

Section 19 Prepositions

A *preposition* helps tell when, where, or how.

- **Prepositions include the words *in, at, under, over, on, through, to, across, around,* and *beside.***
  Jeff left the milk **on** the table.
  He knew it belonged **in** the refrigerator.

- **A *prepositional phrase* is a group of words that includes a preposition and its object. In the sentence below, *in* is the preposition and *minutes* is the object of the preposition.**
  Jeff knew his mother would be home **in five minutes**.

Section 20 Objects

A *direct object* is the word or words that receive the action of the verb. Direct objects follow action verbs. To find the direct object, say the verb followed by "Whom?" or "What?" A direct object is always a noun or pronoun.

> Jacques painted a **picture.**
> (Painted *whom* or *what?* Picture. Picture is the direct object.)

A sentence with a direct object may also have an *indirect object.* An indirect object usually tells to whom something is given.

> Jacques gave his **mom** the painting.

Section 21 Conjunctions

The words *and, or,* and *but* are *conjunctions.*

- **Conjunctions may be used to join words within a sentence.**
  My favorite reptiles are snakes **and** lizards.
  Najim doesn't like snakes **or** lizards.
  He thinks reptiles are cute **but** dumb.

- **Conjunctions can be used to join two or more sentences. When using a conjunction to join sentences, put a comma before the conjunction. (The conjunction *and* does not need a comma if both sentences are short.)**
  I like amphibians, **but** Najim thinks they are creepy.
  We could visit a snake farm next, **or** we could go somewhere else.
  I waited **and** I waited.

Usage

Section 22 Negatives

A *negative word* says "no" or "not."

- **Often negatives are in the form of contractions.**
  Do **not** enter that room.   **Don't** even go near the door.

- **In most sentences it is not correct to use two negatives.**

  Incorrect   Correct
  We **can't** see **nothing**.   We **can't** see anything.
  We **haven't** got **no** solution.   We **haven't** got a solution.

Section 23 Comparisons

- **To compare two people, places, or things, add *-er* to short adjectives and adverbs.**
  An elephant is **tall**. A giraffe is **taller**.
  A lion runs **fast**. A cheetah runs **faster**.

- **To compare three or more items, add *-est* to short adjectives and adverbs.**
  The giraffe is the **tallest** land animal.
  The cheetah is the **fastest** animal alive.

- **When comparing two or more things using the ending *-er* or *-est*, never use the word *more*.**

  Incorrect   Correct
  She is **more faster** than he is.   She is **faster** than he is.

- **The word *more* is used with longer adjectives to compare two persons, places, or things. Use the word *most* to compare three or more persons, places, or things.**
  Mario is **excited** about the field trip.
  Duane is **more excited** than Mario.
  Kiki is the **most excited** student of all.

- **Sometimes the words *good* and *bad* are used to compare. These words change forms in comparisons.**

  Mario is a **good** athlete.   The basketball court is in **bad** shape.
  Kiki is a **better** athlete.   The tennis court is in **worse** shape than
                                     the basketball court.
  Bill is the **best** athlete of all.   The ice rink is in the **worst** shape of all.
  Note: Use *better* or *worse* to compare two things. Use *best* or *worst* to compare three or more things.

Section 24 Contractions

When two or more words are combined to form one word, one or more letters are dropped and replaced by an apostrophe. These words are called *contractions*.

- **In the contraction below, an apostrophe takes the place of the letters *wi*.**
  he will = he'll

- **Here are some other contractions.**

  cannot/can't   have not/haven't   she would/she'd
  could not/couldn't   I will/I'll   they have/they've
  does not/doesn't   it is/it's   we are/we're

Section 25 Plural Nouns

- **A *singular noun* names one person, place, or thing.**
  girl   pond   arrow   donkey

- **A *plural noun* names more than one person, place, or thing. To make most singular nouns plural, add *s*.**
  girl<u>s</u>   pond<u>s</u>   arrow<u>s</u>   donkey<u>s</u>

- **For nouns ending in *sh, ch, x,* or *z*, add *es* to make the word plural.**
  bush/bush<u>es</u>   box/box<u>es</u>
  lunch/lunch<u>es</u>   quiz/quizz<u>es</u>

- **For nouns ending in a consonant and *y*, change the *y* to *i* and add *es*.**
  penny/penn<u>ies</u>   army/arm<u>ies</u>

- **For nouns that end in *f* or *fe*, replace *f* or *fe* with *ves* to make the noun plural.**
  shelf/shel<u>ves</u>   wife/wi<u>ves</u>

- **Some words change spelling when the plural is formed.**
  man/men   woman/women   mouse/mice   goose/geese

- **Some words have the same singular and plural form.**
  deer   sheep   rice

Section 26 Possessives

A *possessive* shows ownership.

- **To make a singular noun possessive, add an apostrophe and *s*.**
  John<u>'s</u> bat   the girl<u>'s</u> bike

- **When a singular noun ends in *s*, add an apostrophe and *s*.**
  Ross<u>'s</u> project   James<u>'s</u> glasses

- **To make a plural noun possessive, add an apostrophe.**
  the soldiers<u>'</u> songs   the girls<u>'</u> bikes

- **When a plural noun does not end in *s*, add an apostrophe and *s*.**
  the men<u>'s</u> ideas   the children<u>'s</u> shoes

Section 27 Problem Words

These words are often misused in writing.

sit	*Sit* means "rest or stay in one place." Sit down and relax for a while.
sat	*Sat* is the past tense of *sit.* I sat in that chair yesterday.
set	*Set* is a verb meaning "put." Set the chair here.

	A, an, and *the* are articles.
a	*A* is usually used before a singular noun beginning with a consonant. a wagon a bicycle a ruler
an	*An* is usually used before a singular noun that begins with a vowel. an article an igloo an orangutan
the	*The* can be used before a singular or plural noun. the ocean the birds the people

may	*May* is used to ask permission or to express a possibility. May I have another hot dog? I may borrow that book someday.
can	*Can* shows that someone is able to do something. I can easily eat three hot dogs.

is	Use *is* to tell about one person, place, or thing. Alabama is warm during the summer.
are	Use *are* to tell about more than one person, place, or thing. Also use *are* with the word *you.* Seattle and San Francisco are cool during the summer. You are welcome to visit me anytime.

doesn't	The contraction *doesn't* is used with the singular pronouns *he, she,* and *it.* He doesn't like sauerkraut. It doesn't agree with him.
don't	The contraction *don't* is used with the plural pronouns *we* and *they.* *Don't* is also used with *I* and *you.* They don't like swiss cheese. I don't care for it, either.

I	Use the pronoun *I* as the subject of a sentence. When using *I* with another noun or pronoun, always name yourself last. I am going to basketball camp. Renée and I will ride together.
me	Use the pronoun *me* after action verbs. Renée will call me this evening. Also use *me* after a preposition, such as *to, at,* and *with.* Pass the ball to me. Come to the game with Renée and me.

good well	*Good* is an adjective. *Well* is an adverb. These words are often used incorrectly. **Incorrect:** Renée plays good. **Correct:** Renée is a good basketball player. She plays well.

let	*Let* is a verb that means "allow." Please let me go to the mall with you.
leave	*Leave* is a verb that means "go away from" or "let stay." We will leave at noon.　　　　　　Leave your sweater here.
was	*Was* is a past-tense form of *be*. Use *was* to tell about one person or thing. Hana was sad yesterday.
were	*Were* is also a past-tense form of *be*. Use *were* to tell about more than one person or thing. Also use the word *were* with *you*. Hana and her friend were both unhappy.　　Were you home yesterday?
has	Use *has* to tell about one person or thing. Rory has a stamp collection.
have	Use *have* to tell about more than one. Also use *have* with the pronoun *I*. David and Lin have a rock collection.　　I have a bottle cap collection.

Section 28 Homophones

Homophones sound alike but have different spellings and meanings.

are	*Are* is a form of the verb *be*.	We are best friends.
our	*Our* is a possessive noun.	Our favorite color is green.
hour	An *hour* is sixty minutes.	Meet me in an hour.
its	*Its* is a possessive pronoun.	The horse shook its shaggy head.
it's	*It's* is a contraction of the words *it is*.	It's a beautiful day for a ride.

there	*There* means "in that place." Please put the books there.
their	*Their* is a possessive pronoun. It shows something belongs to more than one person or thing. Their tickets are in my pocket.
they're	*They're* is a contraction made from the words *they are*. They're waiting for me inside.

two	*Two* is a number.	Apples and pears are two fruits I like.
to	*To* means "toward."	I brought the pot to the stove.
too	*Too* means "also."	I'd like some lunch, too.
	Too can mean "more than enough."	That's too much pepper!

your	*Your* is a possessive pronoun. Where are your socks?
you're	*You're* is a contraction made from the words *you are*. You're coming with us, aren't you?

whose	*Whose* is a possessive pronoun. Whose raincoat is this?
who's	*Who's* is a contraction made from the words *who* and *is* or *who* and *has*. Who's at the front door?　　　　Who's got the correct time?

Writing a Letter

Section 29 Friendly Letters

A *friendly letter* is an informal letter written to a friend or family member.

In a friendly letter, you might send a message, invite someone to a party, or thank someone for a gift. A friendly letter has five parts.

- The *heading* gives your address and the date.
- The *greeting* includes the name of the person you are writing to.
- The *main part* of the letter, or the *body*, gives your message.
- The *closing* is a friendly or polite way to say good-bye.
- The *signature* is your name.

> 35 Rand Street
> Chicago, Illinois 60606
> July 15, 1997
>
> Dear Kim,
>
> Hi from the big city. I'm spending the summer learning to skateboard. My brother Raj is teaching me. He's a pro.
>
> I have one skateboard and hope to buy another one soon. If I can do that, we can practice together when you come to visit.
>
> Your friend,
> *Art*

Section 30 Business Letters

A *business letter* is a formal letter.

You would write a business letter to a company, an employer, a newspaper, or any person you do not know well. A business letter looks a lot like a friendly letter, but a business letter includes the name and address of the business you are writing to.

> 35 Rand Street
> Chicago, Illinois 60606
> July 15, 1997
>
> Swenson Skateboard Company
> 10026 Portage Road
> Lansing, Michigan 48091
>
> Dear Sir or Madam:
>
> Please send me your latest skateboard catalog. I am particularly interested in your newest models, the K-7 series.
> Thank you.
>
> Sincerely yours,
> *Arthur Quinn*
> Arthur Quinn

Section 31 Addressing Letters

The envelope below shows how to address a letter. A friendly letter and a business letter are addressed the same way.

> Arthur Quinn
> 35 Rand St.
> Chicago, IL 60606
>
>   Kim Lee
>   1555 Montague Blvd.
>   Memphis, TN 38106

Guidelines for Listening and Speaking

Section 32 Listening

These steps will help you be a good listener:

- **Listen carefully** when others are speaking.

- **Keep in mind your reason for listening.** Are you listening to learn about a topic? To be entertained? To get directions? Decide what you should get out of the listening experience.

- **Look directly at the speaker.** Doing this will help you concentrate on what he or she has to say.

- **Do not interrupt** the speaker or talk to others while the speaker is talking.

- **Ask questions** when the speaker is finished talking if there is anything you did not understand.

Section 33 Speaking

Being a good speaker takes practice. These guidelines can help you become an effective speaker:

Giving Oral Reports

- **Be prepared.** Know exactly what it is that you are going to talk about and how long you will speak. Have your notes in front of you.

- **Speak slowly** and **clearly.** Speak **loudly** enough so everyone can hear you.

- **Look** at your audience.

Taking Part in Discussions

- **Listen** to what others have to say.

- **Disagree politely.** Let others in the group know you respect their point of view.

- **Try not to interrupt** others. Everyone should have a chance to speak.

Topic Index

Unit 1

Unit 2

Unit 3

Unit 4

Unit 5

Language Index